COLLECTED WORKS

VOLU

By the same author

Already published

COLLECTED WORKS VOLUME TWO
The Alfred Jarry Theatre
Two Stage Scenarios and Two Production Plans
Reviews
On Literature and the Plastic Arts

COLLECTED WORKS VOLUME THREE
Scenarios on the Cinema
Interviews
Letters

COLLECTED WORKS VOLUME FOUR
The Theatre and Its Double
Seraphim's Theatre
The Cenci
Documents on 'The Theatre and Its Double'
Documents on 'The Cenci'

THE CENCI (a play)

THE THEATRE AND ITS DOUBLE (essays)

THE DEATH OF SATAN AND OTHER MYSTICAL WRITINGS (essays)

In preparation

COLLECTED WORKS VOLUME FIVE
Héliogabale
The New Revelations of Being
Correspondence with André Breton

COLLECTED WORKS VOLUME SIX
On Topical Problems
Two Articles For *Voilà*
Private Notes
Satan
Notes On Oriental, Greek And Indian Cultures and Mexico And Civilisation
Revolutionary Statements:
Three Lectures Given At The University Of Mexico City
Mexico
Franz Hals, Ortiz Monasterio, Maria Izquierdo
Letters

VAN GOGH: THE SUICIDED MAN

ANTONIN ARTAUD

COLLECTED WORKS

VOLUME ONE

translated by Victor Corti

CORRESPONDENCE WITH JACQUES RIVIÈRE

UMBILICAL LIMBO

NERVE SCALES

ART AND DEATH

UNPUBLISHED PROSE AND POETRY

CUP AND BALL

SEVEN LETTERS

APPENDIX

JOHN CALDER
LONDON

Originally published in Great Britain 1968
by Calder & Boyars Ltd.,

Originally published in France as *Antonin Artaud: Oeuvres Complètes, Tome 1* by Librairie Gallimard, Paris 1956.

This edition reprinted 1999 by John Calder Publishers

ISBN 0 7145 0169 7 cased
ISBN 0 7145 0170 0 paper

Printed and bound in Canada
by Webcom Limited

CONTENTS

ART AND DEATH

PART TWO

UNPUBLISHED PROSE AND POETRY

CUP AND BALL

APPENDIX

INTRODUCTION

Until publication of this first volume of his *Collected Works*, Antonin Artaud (1896–1948) was chiefly known in English for his work in the theatre, in particular his Theatre of Cruelty. Great as his reversal of stage practice has been (with Brecht he is the leading figure of European theatre in the twentieth century), Artaud was primarily a writer. The pieces reproduced below make it clear that his dramatic activity did not simply overlap into his written work, but that he carried out the same sort of revolution in writing that he did in theatre.

What Artaud proposed was a fundamental reconstruction in thought. He called for destruction of our present social thought patterns and social judgement and their replacement by the unformulated, the intuitive, by individual creation. The latter is of special importance since the author believed there was to be no photocopying in creation. Rather each creative effort must start from fresh premises. Thus he wrote no novels, few plays or short stories and little verse, all of these being set in precast moulds. In contrast to the above are a variety of different compositions, each in its own style and on an extensive range of subjects. By the end of his life Artaud had contributed originating material to motion pictures, travel, the occult, palaeontology, theatre, antiquity and the mind.

He opens on a strident note; an apocalyptic *Preface* that plunges the reader into the heat of the struggle for language. The mind and the flesh are locked in mortal combat over the portals of consciousness. Eschewing letters or even expression, Artaud begins at the beginning —with the utterance of a word, one word that distinguishes man from the animals. Then, less like letters than appeals, less like appeals than the cries of a man exiled on the great plains of the mind, the volume's chronology begins with the *Correspondence with Jacques Rivière.*

Artaud had written to Rivière, not because the latter was editor of the foremost journal in Europe, *La Nouvelle Revue Française,* but because he was respected as the author of two studies on the literature of the Self, *Rimbaud* (1913) and *Thanks to Dada* (1920). In them, Rivière, who had studied Freud and championed the psychological novel, outlined the dangers of the individual identifying himself with his theme. He foresaw the "dead end" to which the subject of the Self would ultimately lead Dada, plotting a progression from Baudelaire and Mallarmé to Breton and Tzara. Hence his warning to his young correspondent not to be enticed by Dada, the journey into that realm being both short and deadly:

"No more painters, no more scribblers, no more musicians, no more sculptors, no more religions, no more royalists, no more radicals, no more imperialists, no more anarchists, no more socialists, no more communists, no more proletariat, no more democrats, no more republicans, no more middle-class, no more aristocrats, no more arms, no more police, no more nations, an end at last to all this stupidity, nothing left, nothing at all, nothing, nothing."[1]

Better stick to events and facts, Rivière advised, to reporting what Artaud saw in others, to objective detail and the "blessed opacity" of reality. But his advice was nothing more than his own position with regard to creation. Besides, we should observe he had misread the *Correspondence,* at least Artaud's part of it, for his young interlocutor bitterly complained he could not even begin to journey into his conscious self owing to the physical obstacles placed in the way of his thought.

This cruel situation, which Artaud considered as an exemplary phenomenon, never allowed him to indulge in self-pity. He continued to record the guerilla warfare

[1] Dada Manifesto.

that went on within him, his nerves constantly sniping at his thoughts. He is ecstatic when even one word comes through unscathed. There was no literature in these letters, but for different reasons than those proposed by Dada. And writing that was not literature clearly troubled Rivière. These words struggling to escape—from what? A gulf yawns before the reader, the gulf that frightened Rivière, as Artaud points out.

But despite the friendly warning in the *Correspondence*, he found himself courted by Dada's immediate successor, Surrealism. Its leader, André Breton, offered him the movement's laboratory, the Central Surrealist Research Bureau, as his own. Maurice Nadeau has so well described the extraordinary atmosphere and operations of this "nerve centre" Artaud directed. He began to contribute a remarkable series of polemical articles to the movement's publications, the Open *Letters* and *Addresses* given below. He indulged in automatic writing and much of *Umbilical Limbo* was composed in this manner. But if he made use of Surrealist techniques, his writing remained as personal as ever. A lifelong fascination for the early German and Flemish mystics, a belief in the mysteries of signs and numbers he had acquired during his youth spent in the Middle East, and those interminable journeys along the paths of consciousness itself, within the brain's cells, were the chief programme of his writing. His directives on the *Activities of the Central Surrealist Research Bureau* are more his own ideas than Surrealism: undermining the supposed supremacy of logic—not only Cartesian logic, but *all* logic—meant giving the mind a chance to create outside any presupposed rules. He defined a Surrealist as a man who "despairs of attaining his own mind". No need to say that man was Artaud. A man who had attained his own mind had made up his mind and henceforth his thought became stratified, precluding unfamiliar creation. Such a man could only constantly reproduce variations of his mind *as he had already attained it*. His mind now became a figure of marble. Having laid down his own Surrealist philosophy in his directives, Artaud met with a glacial reception from the movement's committee. Breton in particular, despite his appreciation of Artaud's "great gifts" as a writer, saw his own position as theoretician of the movement to be threatened. With the support of the committee, he viciously attacked Artaud in the pamphlet *In the Open*, charging the latter with bestiality, excessive cruelty and savagery in his works. Certainly Artaud went much further in his attacks on society than the other Surrealists; compositions such as *Letter to the Legislator of the Drug Act* and *General Security: the Liquidation of Opium* are not empty vituperation. He related man's desire for change, the craving for a solution to the conflict between his physical and intellectual natures. Only a continual, personal Revolution could attempt to resolve that conflict. The painter, André Masson, was alone among the Surrealists to approach Artaud in his intuitive grasp of the nature of the cruelty inherent in that conflict. Masson was the most successful practitioner of automatic art, wherein the landscape of the subconscious became related in strange perspectives to physical elements. *Surrealist Text* is Artaud's account of such work. But having broken with Surrealism, Masson went to live on the outskirts of the capital, in the neighbourhood of the city's principal abattoirs. For several years he painted inside the slaughterhouses, producing works of unrivalled cruelty mingled with powerful eroticism, works that have had such great effect on present artists, a notable example being the British cartoonist, G. Scarfe.

The honeymoon with Surrealism was soon over: Breton and his committee had thrown the weight of the movement behind the French Communist Party. To Artaud this was a betrayal of Surrealism's universality. He accused Breton and the others, in the broadside *In the Dark*, of harnessing Surrealism's liberating nature to a "eunuch's revolution", a proletarian revolution that was no Revolution at all, just transferring power. It should be noted this is not a political attitude on his part; rather he maintained that Surrealism's strength lay in its extra-political position, and it is significant that Breton himself (but not most of the other leading Surrealists) later abjured Communism.

In the 1920's Artaud was accused of introducing anarchy into theatre and certainly his Alfred Jarry Theatre, formed in collaboration with playwright Roger Vitrac (*Manifesto in Plain Terms*) and painter Jean de Bosschère (*The Personal Automaton*), produced a type of theatre that seemed close to anarchy.[1] Yet the theatre Manifestos that appear throughout his *Collected Works* give the lie to this charge. Artaud always built on known, if primitive, models and emphasised a systematic approach. Nor can he be charged with co-operative anarchy. The Surrealists shared their experiences and wrote committee works just as had the Dadaists, but Artaud's contributions to such works are so personal as to rule out any co-operative effort. The beautiful *Letter to the Clairvoyante* was to be such a common undertaking; an appreciation of the young, haunting Mme Sacco, whose turbaned face looks out at the reader from the pages of Breton's *Nadja* (1928). Artaud contrasted Mme Sacco's ethereal existence with his own cruel condition. There is little Surrealism in this letter; rather it points up the fact that the Surrealists gathered under their aegis almost any artists whose own rebellion was clearly enough stated. And the essay, in which Artaud's "great gifts" are displayed for all to see, places him in company with another great contemporary prose poet, Louis Aragon.

Incendiary though much of Artaud's work is, none of the pieces in this volume can be said to exhibit those excesses with which he was charged by his critics. From Rivière on, there was an inclination to pass Artaud off as talented but crazy, in varying degrees of seriousness. The reader may judge the proof of Artaud's sanity from his letters to doctors Soulié de Morant and René Allendy. He had consulted the former because he hoped to find relief for his nervous condition in Chinese acupuncture,

[1] His early theatre theory will be found in the article, *The Evolution of Decor.*

on which Soulié de Morant (besides being a fourth-rate novelist) was a great authority. Allendy and his wife Yvonne, to whom Artaud addressed letters in the spring of 1929, were very different. In the letter dated 30 November, 1927, Artaud defends himself against the doctor's psychoanalysis and insists on the disorder in his physical condition. As his consultant, Allendy knew Artaud was a neuropath and prescribed drugs for his condition, including morphine. But as an experimental analyst, he could not escape his interest in Artaud as a case-book patient. The author of several noted books on Dreams and the Mind, René Allendy also wrote studies on the occult such as his *Symbolism of Numbers* and *Paracelcus*. With his wife, he composed an engrossing work on *Capitalism and Sexuality*. Typical of his frank relations with women (as can be seen in the *Domestic Letters* addressed to his fiancée, Génica Athanasiou) was Artaud's friendship with Yvonne Allendy; she acted as his literary agent and was the business manager of the Alfred Jarry Theatre. He was rather a protegé of hers, and she and her husband were his patrons in Parisian society.

The peculiarities of Artaud's life and work still disturb us now as much as they did at his death, for their nature makes it difficult to approach them with any degree of calm. Artaud has already been subject to attacks in press and radio; the Beats adopted him as a hipster; a stage director introducing his works called him a raving lunatic; finally, critics try to stunt the power of his work by limiting it to a seminal influence, calling it potential, not action. The best approach to his work, however, is in its application to the present. His aim was to extend consciousness into realms previously considered unknowable, such as death and our primal origins. Into the treacherous regions of drugs and magic. He believed liberation of the subconscious and full realisation of the nature of cruelty would enable us to know ourselves. This self-knowledge was to produce a revolution in thought, because its liberating effect was not to be restricted to the arts but must embrace everything. Throughout this book he insists time and again on unlevelling thought; and this is the real purpose behind the first volume of his works. It is the initial step in his revolution. Once this unlevelling has been accomplished creation can begin; its elements are given in the successive volumes.

VICTOR CORTI

PREFACE

Since this is an edition of my complete works, by rights the text of my first published book, "The Heavens at Backgammon", should appear below. This was a collection of poetry which appeared in 1922 through the good offices of my friend Kanhweiler, the publisher and art dealer. On second thoughts, however, I would rather it did not. This short book of poems is in fact not typical of me at all. This is not to say there are occasional lines not altogether worthless or that do not contain a certain audacity of their own.

Witness this short quatrain:

> She who sleeps in my bed
> Sharing the air in my rooms
> Can cast dice on the table
> The very heavens of my mind.

Only they have a rather faded ring, like work by Marie Laurencin, Dignimont, Utrillo, Francis Carco, André Salmon or Raoul Dufy, stylishly styleless witticisms, which I believe originated with Matisse, as if confessing enthusiastic incapability, like a dandy having his shirt cuffs starched with only a severed trunk for a collar.

Furthermore, they contain the troublesome affectations of a style which began to surface towards the end of the other war, 1914–1918, but became so removed from itself that it forgot its own entity long before this last war began.

I consciously thought of this style as making a poem acceptable to the *Mercure de France*, the *Cahiers d'Art*, *Action*, *Commerce* and above all and especially to the sacrosanct *N.R.F.* edited by Jacques Rivière, which never compromised with what I might term a certain Delft Vermeerish or even Leonardo da Vinci-ish aspect of poetry. Not a style but a state of mind.

No, in deciding what constituted poetry, Jacques Riviére did not have the fault of considering treatment first above all else, that is, *his* poetry, although he had a special liking for baldly well-made poems. The word skeleton lifts its cloak, opens out over the rag-cloak of lately desired and soon destroyed language. I do not think he cared whether poems were devoid of feeling or meaning, but he was very fond of trinkets in which minds quivered, bitter almonds out of trinkets destroyed by speech.

This is the text of the letter I received about September 1923 from Jean Paulhan, who was his secretary at the time:

"Dear Sir,

Enclosed please find your poems which I found full of charm. Jacques Rivière does not appear to have found their charm either uniform enough, or self-assured enough as yet."

In deference to this letter I continued for a further month to work at writing a verbally, not a grammatically, successful poem.

Then I gave up. As far as I was concerned, the problem was not to find out what might manage to worm its way into the strictures of written language,

but into the web of my living soul.

By which words entered like knives in lasting carnation,

a fitting, dying in-carnation under a span, the burning island of a gallows lantern.

I mean whose flesh gleams red, opaque, obdurate, empty as wind, proliferating uses, temptingly acid,

words which would enable me to enter the grain of this grim flesh, (I say GRIM, meaning underhand, but in Greek it is called *tavaturi* and *tavaturi* means noise, etc.).

Flesh to be blooded under the hammer,

to be extirpated with knives.

Thus I did not manage to infuse my web into these abortive poems,

to insert into their words, not my soul, Oh, not my soul but the *pressure* in me, the darkness of my congenital tension, of my excessive, arid oppression.

I am innately genital and if we examine what that means closely, it means I never made the most of myself.

There are some fools who think of themselves as beings, as innately being.

I am he who, in order to be, must whip his innateness.

One who must be a being innately, that is always whipping this sort of non-existent kennel, O! bitches of impossibility.

Thus the tenor of the poems in this unsuccessful book were like those rejected by Jacques Rivière for the *N.R.F.* and about which I wrote him the letters below.

I am not a critic, like Brunetière or Benjamin Crémieux, able to rate the sort of work I produced in writing these letters or whether it is true I took up the entire problem of poetic inspiration and its words,

(and its words. What is that? Its words are called prosody, so they say,)

once again in writing of these phenomena.

(This last sentence was written with fly droppings:

flies; rhinitis or synovia; my unconscious was about to say Segovia because it rhymes with phenomena. A snuff-like phrase, fallen from the nose of a cur in confinement, who did not insinuate it, but I uttered it over his being, since his birth was not a shining event for him.)

Inspiration is nothing but a foetus and the word is also nothing but a foetus. I know when I wanted to write, words failed me, that's all.

I never knew anything else.

And I just don't give a damn whether my sentences sound like French or Papuan.

But if I drive a point home, a violent word, I want it to suppurate in the sentence like a hundred-gashed laceration. If a word is obscene, no one holds it against the author because of its obscenity, but they hold it against him if it is gratuitous, I mean prosaic and flat.

Thought underlies grammar, an infamy harder to conquer, an infinitely more shrewdish maid, rougher to override when taken as an innate fact.

For thought is a matron who has not always existed.

But let my life's inflated words inflate themselves through living in the b-a-b-a of composition. I am writing for illiterates.

When a poet cries out, it may perhaps mean a tasty dish for infinity, but that dish must be cooked in . . . etc., etc.

Under the crushed, bitter bladder lay the corpse of a dead man. Jacques Rivière was his name, at the start of a strange life, mine.

Thus Jacques Rivière refused my poems but not the letters with which I pulled them to pieces. And it always seemed strange to me that he died shortly after publishing these letters.

For I went to see him one day and told him the underlying meaning in the letters, in the heart of the marrow of the writer, Antonin Artaud.

And I asked him if it had been understood.

I felt his heart swell up as if it would burst when confronted with the problem.

He told me it had not been understood.

I would not be surprised if the black cyst which opened up within him that day, drew him away from life much more than his own sickness.

Words are a morass explained, not by existence, but by man's suffering.

As a poet I hear words that do not belong to the world of ideas.

For where I am there is no more thinking.

Freedom is just a convention and even more unbearable than slavery.

And cruelty is an idea in practice.

Fleshy colour, incarnate in bony will-power, upon sinews of suppressed will-power,

my voices are not called Titania,

Ophelia, Beatrice, Ulysses, Morella or Ligea,

Aeschylus, Hamlet or Panthesilea,

they are bruised by hostile sarcophagi, the seething of burnt flesh,

aren't they Sonia Mossé.

There are two or three coffins in my past I can now no longer forgive anyone, no more than I will forgive the Roman church for having baptised me against my will.

So when I say I renounce baptism, I not only renounce it as baptism, but as the awful masturbation of an idea.

A headlong fall into the flesh, deprived of calling cruelty permanent, either cruelty or freedom.

Theatre is the block, the gibbet, the trenches, the crematorium or the madhouse.

Cruelty, mangled bodies.

Railing *within* the black cyst which one day cured me of thinking.

Once I had three daughters strangled and they will return from the black cyst:

Germaine, Yvonne and Neneka.

Germaine Artaud strangled at seven months, watched me from St. Peter's cemetery in Marseilles, until the day in 1931 when, in the middle of the Dôme in Montparnasse, I had the impression she was nearby, watching me.

Yvonne Allendy died with suspicious marks on her neck, and her belly was swollen like a person who had really drowned, only there was no river nearby.

Neneka Chilé died with suspicious bruises on her neck and one shoulder strangely contorted.

The cane of "The New Revelations of Being" fell into the black cyst along with the little sword.

I have got another cane ready to accompany my collected works in hand to hand combat, not with ideas, but with those monkeys who never stop riding them to death from one end of my conscious self to the other, as well as through my organism they have blighted.

For the things which go ploc-ploc in my genitals are not ideas but beings and I will not stand universal sexuality that endlessly saps and sheaths me from head to toe.

My cane will be this furious book called forth by ancient peoples now dead, spotted throughout my nervous fibres like daughters shed.

ANTONIN ARTAUD

PART ONE

CORRESPONDENCE WITH JACQUES RIVIÈRE

I

Jacques Rivière to Antonin Artaud

1 May 1923

Dear Sir,

I regret I am unable to publish your poems in the *Nouvelle Revue Française*. However, I found them sufficiently interesting to want to make the acquaintance of their author. If it is convenient for you to call at our offices any Friday between four and six, I would be happy to see you.

Yours sincerely,

Jacques Rivière.

Antonin Artaud to Jacques Rivière

5 June 1923

Dear Sir,

At the risk of troubling you, will you allow me to hark back to some of the terms of this afternoon's conversation.

For the question of the admissibility of these poems is a problem which concerns you as much as me. Of course, I am talking about their ultimate acceptance, their literary existence.

I suffer from a fearful mental disease. My thought abandons me at every stage. From the mere fact of thought itself to the external fact of its materialisation in words. Words, the forms of phrases, inner directions of thought, the mind's simplest reactions, I am in constant pursuit of my intellectual being. Thus, when *I am able to grasp a form*, however imperfect, I hold on to it, afraid to lose all thought. As I know I do not do myself justice, I suffer from it, but I accept it in fear of complete death.

This is all very badly expressed and risks interjecting

a dangerous misunderstanding in your judgement of me.

Therefore, out of respect for the principal feeling which dictates my poems and those keener ideas and expressions I hit upon, I still offer these poems to the world. I felt and accepted these expressions, these poorly written phrases you reproached me for. Remember, I did not question them. They came from the deep insecurity of my thoughts. I am only too happy when this insecurity is not replaced by the complete non-existence I sometimes suffer.

Here, too, I am afraid you will misunderstand me. I would like you to understand clearly it is not a matter of the sort of partial-existence which comes from what is commonly called inspiration, but from total abstraction, from true wastage.

This is also why I told you I had nothing further, no work in the offing, the few things I submitted to you being the vestiges of what I was able to salvage from the utter void.

It is very important to me that the few manifestations *of mental* existence I have been able to give myself should not be dismissed as non-existent, because of flaws and poorly written phrases scattered through them.

In submitting them to you, it seemed to me their defects and unevenness were not gross enough to destroy each poem's overall impression.

Please believe me, Sir, I have no immediate, petty goal in mind, I only want to settle a crucial problem.

For I cannot hope time or hard work will set these lapses and unintelligibility to rights. This is the reason why I find it so important and am so concerned to lay claim, even to this abortive existence. And the question I would like answered is: do you think one can grant less literary truth and power to a poem which is imperfect but full of great beauty, than to a perfect poem without much inner excitement in it? I admit a magazine like the *Nouvelle Revue Française* requires a certain set standard and great purity of content, but aside from these, is the substance of my thoughts so tangled and its overall beauty so devitalised by the faltering and impurities which run through them, they *literarily* do not succeed in coming alive? The whole problem of my ideas is at stake. And for my part the question is nothing less than knowing whether or not I have the right to go on thinking, either in prose or poetry.

One of these coming Fridays may I take the liberty of offering you, as a token of my esteem, a little booklet of poems Mr. Kahnweiler has just published, entitled *The Heavens at Backgammon*, as well as a slim volume in the Contemporaries Collection, *Twelve Songs*. You could then write me your *definitive* appreciation of my poems.

Antonin Artaud

Jacques Rivière to Antonin Artaud

23 June 1923

Dear Mr. Artaud,

I carefully read what you were good enough to submit for my opinion and in all sincerity I can reassure you concerning the misgivings apparent in your letter, by which I was very touched, since you chose me as confidant. I told you from the first, there are awkward passages and disconcerting oddities in your poems. But they seem to me allied with a certain enquiry on your part, rather than lack of command over your ideas.

Obviously (and this is what stops me for the time being publishing any of your poems in the *Nouvelle Revue Française*), you have not generally achieved a sufficiently unified impression. But I am experienced enough in reading manuscripts to get an idea that this concentration of your talents focused on a simple poetic objective is not at all closed to you by nature of your temperament. With a little patience, even if this simply means cutting out some of the divergent imagery or traits, you will be able to write perfectly coherent, harmonious poems.

I will always be delighted to see you, to chat with you and read anything you would like to submit. Should I return the copy you brought me?

Yours very sincerely,

Jacques Rivière

II

Antonin Artaud to Jacques Rivière

Paris, 29 January 1924

Dear Sir,

You have just cause to have forgotten me. Last May, I had mentally confessed to you a little. I had asked you a question. Will you allow me to complete this confession now, to resume it, to plumb my inmost depths. I am not attempting to justify myself in your eyes, as it makes little difference to me whether I appear to exist to anyone. I have the whole distance separating me from myself to cure me of other people's opinions. Please do not regard this as insolence, but rather as a true admission, the painful statement of a distressing state of mind.

I resented your reply for some time. I had presented myself to you as a mental case, an actual psychic anomaly and your reply was a literary opinion about poems I did not care about, I could not care about. I flattered myself you had not understood me. Now I see perhaps I was not explicit enough and kindly forgive me for this as well.

I fancied I had captured your attention, if not with the affectation of my verse, then at least by the rarity of certain phenomena of an intellectual order. This explicitly caused these poems not to be, could not be different than they were, despite the ability within me to polish them to the utmost perfection. A conceited statement, a boast, but an intentional one.

In fact, my query may have been specious but I put the question to you, to you and no one else, because of your mind's extreme sensitivity, its almost morbid penetration. I flattered myself in thinking I was bringing you a case, a distinctive mental case, and as I believed you to be interested in any form of mental malformation, in all the obstacles which destroy thought, at the same time I hoped to draw your attention to the *real*, the incipient value of my thought and my mind's compositions.

This diffusion in my poems, these defective forms, this constant falling off in my ideas, must not be set down to lack either of practice or control of the instrument I was manipulating, of *intellectual development*. Rather to a focal collapse of my soul, a kind of essential and fugitive erosion in thought, to a transitory non-possession of physical gain to my development, to the abnormal separation of the elements of thought (the impulse to think at every stratifying endpoint of thought, by way of every condition, through all the branchings in thought and form).

There is, therefore, one single thing which destroys my ideas. Something which does not stop me being what I might, but if I may express it thus, leaves me in a state of suspense. Something furtive which robs me of the words *I have found*, which reduces my terseness of mind, progressively destroying the bulk of my ideas within its own matter. It even deprives me of the recollection of those turns of phrase by which we express ourselves and that render the most inseparable, the most localised and most live cadences of thought. I won't labour the point. I do not need to describe my state of mind.

I would only like to say enough for you to finally believe and understand me.

And give me credit. I beg you, please admit the reality of these phenomena, admit their furtiveness, their endless recurrence, admit I would have written this letter earlier if I had not been in this state. Therefore I will repeat my question once more.

You know how subtle, how delicately balanced the mind is, don't you? Have I not told you enough to prove I have a mind which *literarily* exists, just as T exists, or E or S or M? Give my mind back its power of concentration, its missing cohesion, its uniform terseness, the consistency of its own matter. (And objectively speaking this is very little.) Then tell me if what is missing in my (former) poems could not be put back in them in one fell swoop.

Do you think that in a sound mind, excitement goes hand in hand with extreme weakness, or that one can both surprise and disappoint? Finally, if I have understood my mind well, I can only appraise its compositions in so far as they merge with it in a sort of blissful unconsciousness. This will be my criterion.

To conclude, I therefore enclose my mind's latest creation. It is not worth much in relation to myself, however it is none the less better than nothing. It is a makeshift. But my problem is to know whether it is better to write this or nothing at all.

You can answer this by either accepting or refusing this short attempt. You will judge it from an absolute standpoint. But I can tell you it would be a very great consolation to me to think that, while my *whole* being is not as lofty, as profound or as comprehensive as me, I can still be something. For this reason, Sir, please be really conclusive. Please judge this letter aside from any question of trends, concepts, personal taste, weigh it against the charity in your soul, the characteristic lucidity of your mind. Think it over with your heart.

It probably points to an intellect, a living soul, to which a certain place is due. On behalf of this soul's manifest irradiation, brush it aside only if your conscience protests strongly. But if you are in doubt, please decide in my favour.

I refer the matter to your judgement.

Antonin Artaud

Postcript to a Letter in which some of Jacques Rivière's literary theories were discussed

You might answer: to advise me on such matters, another sort of insight and mental cohesiveness are needed. Well, my weakness and my *absurdity* is I must write at all costs and express myself.

I am a man whose mind has greatly suffered and as such I have a *right* to speak. I know what sort of business goes on inside it. I have agreed to yield once and for all to my inferiority. Yet I am not stupid. I know there are broader and perhaps different styles of thought than mine. I am only waiting for my mind to alter, for its upper echelons to open. Perhaps by tomorrow or even in an hour, my thoughts will have changed, but these present thoughts exist, I won't allow my thoughts to be lost.

A. A.

CRY

The little celestial poet
Opens the shutters of his heart,
The skies collide. Lethe
Uproots the symphony.

Groom in the mad house
Given wolves to tend,
Does not suspect the wraths
Smouldering under the vault's
Great suspended bay above.

Thus silence and darkness
Muzzle all adulteration.
The sky, in seven-league boots,
Strides towards the crossroads of sound.

The star eats. The tilted sky
Begins its flight towards the peaks,
Night sweeps up the scraps
Of our gratifying meal.

A slug walks the earth,
Ten thousand whites touch their caps
A slug crawls
Where the earth vanished.

Yet angels, uncalled by obscenity,
Returned in peace
When arose the true voice
Of the summoning spirit.

The sun, lower than day,
Turned the ocean to steam

A strange yet clear dream
Was born on the crumbling earth.

The little lost poet
Leaves his celestial post
With an unearthly idea
Clutched to his shaggy heart.

*

Two traditions met.
But our padlocked thoughts
Were short of space;
Begin again.

A. A.

Antonin Artaud to Jacques Rivière

22 March 1924

My letter at least deserved a reply. Please return letters and manuscripts, Sir.

I would have liked to find something intelligent to say to you to indicate clearly just what separates us, but what is the use. I have an unformed, idiotic mind. Think what you like of me.

Antonin Artaud

Jacques Rivière to Antonin Artaud

Paris, 25 March 1924

Dear Mr. Artaud,

Yes, you are right, your letters deserve a reply. I was not able to send you one, that is all. Please forgive me.

One thing struck me. The contrast between your extraordinarily precise self-analysis and the vague, at least, the unformed nature of your attempted productions.

In the letter I sent you last year, I was no doubt wrong to try and reassure you at all costs. I acted like those doctors who claim to cure their patients by refusing to believe them, by denying the singularity of their case then forcibly trying to bring them back to normal. This is a dangerous method. I am sorry I used it.

Even if I had no other proof than your uneven, faltering, tortured handwriting, as if swallowed up here and there by invisible whirlwinds, this would be enough to confirm the real existence of the phenomena of mental "erosion" you complain of.

But how do you escape them so well when you try to define your difficulty? Could it be because your anxiety gives you the strength and lucidity you lack when you yourself are not involved? Or is it closeness to the object you are trying to grasp which suddenly enables you to grasp it so confidently? In any case, when analysing your own mind you are completely, remarkably successful and this must give you confidence in your reason, since it is also the instrument which finds them for you.

Other considerations may also help you, if not to hope to be cured, then at least to bear your sufferings patiently. These are of a universal nature. Somewhere in your letters you mentioned the "mind's delicate balance". This is more than sufficiently proved by the mental breakdowns psychiatry studies and classifies. But how far so-called normal thought results from the operation of chance, has probably not been shown clearly enough, as yet.

It seems no one today could contest that the mind exists independently, that it tends to feed on its own matter, and that it develops within the individual with a sort of egoism, without worrying about keeping him in time with the world. Paul Valéry staged our autonomous intellectual operations in a wonderful manner in his famous *Evening with Mr. Teste*. By itself, the mind is a sort of canker. It reproduces itself, constantly spreading out in all directions. You noted yourself as one of your torments "the impulse to think at every stratifying endpoint of thought". The mind's outlets are unlimited in number. No ideas stop it, no ideas tire or satisfy it. Even the temporary relief which our physical faculties experience through exercise are unknown to it. A thinking man wears himself out completely. Romanticism aside, there is no other end to pure thought than death.

There is a whole body of literature—I know it preoccupies you as much as it interests me—which is the product of the immediate and, so as to speak, animal operations of the mind. This type of literature has the appearance of a vast field of ruins. The columns still standing are supported by chance alone. Chance reigns there, chance and a sort of dreary multiplicity. One might say it is the clearest and most exact manifestation of the animal nature in all men, but which we usually instinctively try to shackle with the bonds of fact and experience.

But you might say, is that what is meant by the "mind's delicate balance"? While I am complaining about man's weakness, you have described another complaint which seems to me to arise from an excessively forceful, overflowing mind.

Put a little more precisely, my opinion is this. The mind is delicate in as much as it requires hurdles—accidental obstacles. By itself, it goes astray and destroys itself. It seems to me this mental "erosion", this inner pilfering, this "destruction" of thought "within its own matter" affecting you, is caused solely by the excessive freedom you allow it. The absolute is the source of its disorder. To be taut, the mind requires a landmark, an encounter with the blessed opacity of experience. The only cure for madness is the simplicity of facts.

As soon as you accept things on a mental level, you accept all mental disturbances and especially all mental laxity. If we understand thought to mean *creation*, as you seem to most of the time, it must at all costs be relative. Security, strength and tenacity can only be found by involving the mind in something.

I know, there is almost a lightheaded feeling in the instant it radiates pure, in the moment when its stream flows straight from the brain and finds great areas, many spheres and levels where it can spread out. This is the wholly subjective impression of complete freedom, even complete intellectual licence our "Surrealists" have tried to express in the principle of a fourth poetic dimension. But the penalty for these soaring flights is at hand. Universal possibilities are transformed into concrete impossibilities. The impression, once captured, engenders twenty more in revenge which paralyse us and ravage the mind's substance.

Does this mean the mind's normal operations should consist of a slavish imitation of facts and that thinking consists of nothing but reproduction? I do not think so. We must choose what we wish to "express" which should always be not only something definite, not only the knowable, but the unknown as well. For the mind to achieve its greatest strength the concrete should serve as a mystery. Every successful "thought", all language which makes its point, these words by which a writer is later recognised, are always the result of compromise between a stream of intelligence flowing out of him and incomprehension he encounters, surprise, a mental block. The appropriateness of an expression always includes the remnant of an hypothesis. The word must have struck a veiled object but before our reason grasped it. But where the object or obstacle are entirely missing, the mind carries straight on, defective. And everything disintegrates in immense contingency.

Perhaps I am judging you from too abstract a point of view, at the same time as with too personal a bias. None the less, it seems to me your case can largely be explained by the considerations I have just enumerated in a little too much detail, and it falls into the overall scheme I have tried to set out. As long as you let your mental power pour into the absolute, it is buffeted by cross-currents, riddled with incapability, exposed to ravaging blasts which throw it into confusion. But immediately your anxiety brings you back into your own mind and you turn to this familiar yet enigmatic object, it concentrates, sharpens, becomes useful and penetrating and gives you positive help, namely truths expressed with all the relief that allows you to articulate them, and make them understandable to others. Thus, something that transcends your suffering, your very existence, raising you up, strengthening you and bringing you the only reality man can reasonably hope to achieve by his own means, reality in others.

I am not being mulishly optimistic, but I refuse to give you up as lost. My sympathy for you is very great. It was amiss of me not to write to you for so long.

I am keeping your poem. Send me all your future work.

Yours very sincerely,

Jacques Rivière

III

Antonin Artaud to Jacques Rivière

Paris, 7 May 1924

My Dear Mr. Rivière,

To return to a long-standing question, one need only imagine for a moment that this powerlessness in expressing myself applies to the most basic needs in my life, to the most pressing emergencies, and the resultant suffering, to understand I have not given up about myself for lack of trying. I am unattached to poetry. My not fulfilling myself depends entirely on circumstances external and accidental to my ability. All I need is someone to believe I have the potential to crystallize things in appropriate forms and words.

I have had to wait all this time for an occasion to write you this short note which is clear in the absence of being well-written. You can draw the obvious conclusions.

One thing in your letter still seems a little unclear to me. What are you going to do with the poem I sent you? You have put your finger on one side of my nature. Literature, as such, interests me very little. But if you happen to think it worth while publishing, could you please send me the proofs, as I am very anxious to correct two or three words.

Kindest regards,

Antonin Artaud

Jacques Rivière to Antonin Artaud

24 May 1924

Dear Mr. Artaud,

I have been holding out against an idea which occurred to me and which definitely attracts me. I want you to think about it. I hope it will please you. Besides, it still has to be worked out.

Why not publish one, or all of the letters you wrote me? I have just re-read the one dated 29 January. It is really quite remarkable.

It would only require a little substitution. I mean we could give the writer and his correspondent pen names. Perhaps I could even draft a reply based on the one I sent you, but treated at greater length and more impersonal. We might also add lines of your poetry or some of your essay on Uccello, the whole constituting a rather interesting novel in letters.

Let me know what you think of this.

Yours,

Jacques Rivière

Antonin Artaud to Jacques Rivière

25 May 1924

Dear Mr. Rivière

Why lie, why try to put something which is life's very cry on a literary level? Why fictionalize something made from the soul's ineradicable essence, which is like the complaint of reality? Yes, your idea pleases me, I am delighted with it, it fills me with joy, provided we do not give the reader the impression he thinks he is looking at fabricated work. We have the right to lie, but not about the heart of things. I do not want to put my name to the letters. But the reader must definitely think he has the elements of a true story in front of him. We would have to publish my letters from the first to the last, going back to June, 1923. The reader should have all the facts under discussion in front of him.

A man is in possession of his faculties at intervals yet

even so, he never fully achieves self-knowledge. He does not achieve that constant concert of his powers without which all true creativity is impossible. Meanwhile, the man exists. I mean he is a distinct entity and this enhances him. Should he be condemned to oblivion on the pretext he can only give fragments of his self? You yourself do not think so, and the proof is the importance you attach to these fragments. I had long since thought of suggesting we collect them together. I had not dared to do it up to now and your letter responds to my wishes. So you will see how happily I received your suggestion.

I am well aware of the stops and starts in my poems, jolts which are linked with the very essence of inspiration and due to my ingrained inability to concentrate on an object. This is the result of physiological weakness, a weakness linked with the very stuff of what is commonly called the soul, our nervous energy emanating and solidifying around things. Our whole period suffers from this weakness, for example; Tristan Tzara, André Breton, Pierre Reverdy. Only their souls are not physiologically affected, not substantially affected. They are in all matters touching on other things, but not *outside thought.* Where then does this sickness stem from, is it really something in the spirit of the times, a miracle floating in the air, an evil cosmic prodigy or the discovery of a new world, a genuine extension of reality? Nevertheless it is still true they do not suffer and I do, not only mentally but physically, in my everyday soul. This lack of application to an object, a characteristic of all literature, is a lack of application to life in my case. Speaking for myself, I can honestly say I am not in this world and such a statement is not merely an intellectual pose. My latest poems seem to me to show real progress. Are they really so unpublishable in their entirety? Still, this is not important, I prefer to show myself as I am, in my inexistence and uprooted as I am. Anyway we could publish a large number of extracts. I think most of the verses are alright, taken as they are. Their value is only destroyed taken collectively. I leave the choice of extracts up to you and the arrangement of the letters. *I cannot judge that.* What I am most concerned about is that no misunderstanding should creep in on the nature of the phenomena I have evoked in my own defence. The reader must believe in a genuine sickness, not just a phenomenon of the times, in a sickness which is near to the nature of man and his main expressive potential and applicable to a whole life.

A sickness affecting the soul in its most profound reality, poisoning its expression. Spiritual poison. Genuine *paralysis*. Sickness robbing us of speech and memory, and uprooting thought.

I think I have said enough to make myself understood, then publish this last letter. In concluding it, I notice it could serve as a recapitulation and conclusion of our discussion for my part.

Please accept my heart-felt thanks,
Antonin Artaud

Antonin Artaud to Jacques Rivière

6 June 1924

Dear Mr. Rivière

. . . .

My mental life is all shot through with petty doubts and unalterable certainties expressed in clear, coherent language. My weaknesses are more tremulous in texture, themselves larval and ill-formed. They bear living, anguished roots reaching down into the heart of life. But they do not bear life's turmoil, since in them we do not feel the cosmic afflatus of a soul shaken to its foundations. They come from a mind which has not considered its weakness. Otherwise it would spell it out in terse, forceful words. There, my dear Sir, lies the whole problem. To have the inalienable reality, the tangible clarity of feeling within one's self, to have them so deeply they cannot help expressing themselves in richness of language, memorized constructions which could come into play, or be of some use. The moment the soul proposes to coordinate its riches, its discoveries, its relevations, unknowingly at the very minute the thing is about to emanate, a higher vicious will attacks the soul like vitriol, attacks the mass of words and imagery, attacks the mass of our feelings and leaves me as it were panting at the gates of life.

Now supposing I physically felt this will sweep through me. Suppose it jolted me with its sudden, unexpected continuous electricity. Suppose all my conscious moments were shaken on certain days by these deep-seated tornadoes nothing external betrays. Tell me if any literary work is in keeping with such states? What mind could resist them? What personality would not disintegrate under them? If only I had the strength, I would sometimes indulge in the luxury of mentally subjecting any prominent mind, any writer young or old who produces material, whose new-born ideas are listened to, to the mortification of such cruel pain and see what would be left of him. We should never be too hasty in judging men. We should give them credit *ad absurdum*, right down to the last dregs. These rash works which often appear to originate from a mind not yet in possession of itself, which perhaps will never do so, who knows what sort of brain they conceal, what life-force, what fever of ideas circumstances alone have curtailed. Enough about me and my unborn works. I only want to feel my mind.

Antonin Artaud

Jacques Rivière to Antonin Artaud

Paris, 8 June 1924

Dear Mr. Artaud,

Perhaps I somewhat indiscreetly replaced your singularity and suffering with my ideas and prejudices. Perhaps I indulged in table talk when I should have tried to understand and sympathise with you. I wanted to reassure and cure you. This doubtless springs from the sort of rage with which I always react towards life, where I am concerned. In the struggle for life, I would only admit myself beaten when I breathe my last.

Your last letters, in which the word "soul" often takes

the place of the word "mind", evoked my sympathy even more deeply, but embarrassed me more than the earlier ones. I feel I am close to deep and private suffering. I am in suspense in front of sickness I can only dimly perceive. But perhaps this puzzled attitude will encourage you and help you more than my previous rationalisations.

Yet, is there no way for me to understand your torment? You say, "a man is only in possession of his faculties at intervals, and even when he is, he never fully achieves self-knowledge". That man is you. But I can also tell you it is me. I know nothing like your "tornadoes", nor that "vicious will" which "attacks the soul from without", the soul and its powers of expression. But while being more general and less painful, sometimes my feeling of my own inferiority is no less definite.

In order to explain the alternations I go through, like you, I set aside the convenient symbol of inspiration. We are dealing with something deeper, more "substantial", if I may be allowed to distort the meaning of the word, than a happy inspiration which might or might not spring from the depths of the mind. We are dealing with the stages I pass through in my own reality. Unfortunately, not willingly! But in a purely accidental way.

A remarkable thing is that the fact of my existence, as you noted about yourself, is at no time a subject of serious doubt to me. There always remains part of myself, but that part is often something poor, awkward, feeble, almost suspect. At such times, I do not lose all sense of complete reality, but occasionally, I lose all hope of ever regaining it. It is like a roof over my head, held up as if by a miracle, yet I can never build up to it.

My feelings, my ideas—my usual ones—pass through my mind with a slightly weird appearance. They are so weakened, so hypothetical, they seem to be part of a purely philosophical speculation. Yet they are still there. But they look on me as if to make me wonder at their absence.

Proust described the "heart's intermittences". We must now describe the intermittences of being.

There are obvious physiological reasons for these fadings out in the soul, which are often fairly easy to diagnose. You spoke of the soul "as the solidification of our nervous energy". You say it can be "physiologically affected". Like you, I believe it is greatly dependent on the nervous system. Yet its attacks are so erratic, I understand why sometimes we are led to look for a mystical explanation, as you do, in a "vicious will" bent on stunting it from without.

In any case, I believe it is a fact that men of a certain type are prone to fluctuations in their mental level. When we mechanically adopt an habitual psychological attitude, how often have we abruptly discovered it transcends us, or rather have we grown surreptitiously unequal to it! How often has our most normal character suddenly seemed false, or even fictitious, through lack of the mental or "basic" resources which should nourish it!

Where does our being go and whence does it return, when all the psychologists up to now pretend they regard it as a constant? It is an almost insoluble problem without turning to religious dogma like that of Grace, for example. I wonder at our era (I am thinking of Pirandello and Proust, in whom it is implicit) which raised the question without answering it, and so limited itself to anguish.

"A physiologically affected soul." What a terrible heritage. Still, in a certain respect, without regard to insight, it can also be a privilege. It is the only means we have of understanding ourselves a little, at least of looking at ourselves. Whoever has never been depressed, whoever has never felt their souls broken by their bodies, invaded by its weakness, is incapable of appreciating any truth about man. We must go below, we must look at the underside. In order to ascertain, we must no longer be able to move, hope or believe. How could we distinguish our intellectual or moral mechanisms if we were not temporarily deprived of them? This must be a consolation to those who experience death in small doses in this way, for they are the only ones who in some small measure know what life consists of.

Then "the mortification of such cruel pain" prevents the rise of the ridiculous overcast of pride in them. You wrote to me: "I always have the distance separating me from myself to cure me of other people's opinions". Such is the use of this "distance". It "cures us of other people's opinions". It stops us doing anything to attract them, to suit ourselves to them. It keeps us pure and, despite the fluctuations in our real selves, it assures us of a greater degree of personal identity.

Of course, our health is the only acceptable ideal, the only one to which what I call a man has the right to aspire. But when a man has it from the start, it hides half the world from him.

In spite of myself, I have once again let myself try to reassure you, to show you how a "normal state of mind" can be precarious even in matters of existence. I hope with all my heart you find the steps I described attainable, both from an ascending and from the other point of view. After all why should moments of plenitude, of self-assurance, be denied you if you already have the courage to desire them? There is only ultimate danger for those who give in. The only final death is for those who take a liking for death.

My best wishes,

Jacques Rivière

UMBILICAL LIMBO

UMBILICAL LIMBO

Here where others proffer their works, I claim to do nothing more than show my mind.

Life consists of burning up questions.

I do not consider any work apart from life.

I do not like indifferent creativity. Nor do I consider the mind as unconcerned with itself. Each of my works, each outline of my self, each frozen flowering of my inmost soul oozes over me.

I am as much myself in a letter written to explain the inner contraction of my being and the meaningless emasculation of my life, as in an essay outside me, which seems like an indifferent gestation of my mind.

I suffer because the Mind is not in life and life is not Mind. I suffer because the Mind is an organ, the Mind is an interpreter or the Mind intimidates things to accept them in the Mind.

I hold this book up in life, I want it to be attacked by things outside, primarily by all the shearing jolts, all the twitching of *my future ego*.

These pages all float about like icicles in my mind. Thus excuse my complete freedom. I object to any differentiation between the moments of my ego. I do not acknowledge any plan in the mind.

We must get rid of the Mind, just as we must get rid of literature. I say the Mind and life interconnect at all levels. I would like to make a Book to disturb people, like an open door leading them where they would never have gone of their own free will. Simply a door communicating with reality.

This is no more a preface to a book than, say, the poems that stand out in it, or the enumeration of all the furors of soul-sickness.

This too is only an icicle stuck in my throat.

Great thinking, overpopulated ardour bore my ego like a full abyss. A carnal, booming wind blew, heavy with brimstone. Tiny rootlets filled the wind like a network of veins and their switches flashed. The air was measurable and grinding, but had no penetrable form. And its eye was a mosaic of bursts, a sort of hard cosmic hammer distorted by weight, ceaselessly dropping like a brow in space, with a seemingly distilled sound. And the noise's muffled sheath bore the dull entreaty and penetration of a living look. Yes, the air spewed out its full mental padding where no thought was yet clear or able to replenish its unloaded objects. But little by little the mass turned like powerful, slimy nausea, a sort of huge influx of vegetal thundering blood. And the rootlets trembled on the borders of my mind's eye, broke away with dizzy speed from the wind's contracted mass. And all the air shook like sexual organs ransacked by the fiery, heavenly globe. And something like a real dove's beak pierced the confused mass of states of mind, all deep thought stratified at that moment, resolved itself, grew transparent and reduced.

And now we needed a hand which became the grasping organ itself. And the whole vegetal mass revolved two or three more times and each time my eye changed place to a more precise spot. Darkness itself grew more profuse and objectiveless. All frost grew clear.

Beside me hound-god, like a shaft
Its tongue pierces the crust,
The double, vaulted, flattened dome
Of the itching earth.

Here comes the water triangle
Stepping like a bug
But under the burning bug
It rounds as a stab.

Under the bosom of hideous earth
The bitch-god sleeps,
Away from bosom of earth and ice
Rotting its hollow tongue.

Here comes the hammer-virgin,
To crush the earth cellars
Where the stellar dog's skull
Feels the horrible level rise.

Doctor,

There is one point I would like to have stressed: the importance of the thing your injections go to work on. That sort of primal relaxation of my being, that fall in my mental level which does not mean as one might think any slackening in my morality (in my moral soul), or even in my intelligence, but if you like in my serviceable intellect, in my thinking potential, which is more concerned with my feelings about my ego than with what I display to others.

That multiform, secret crystallisation of thought, which chooses its form at *a given moment*. The ego instantly, directly crystallises in the midst of all possible forms, of all modes of thought.

Now Doctor, since you now have all the facts on what can be affected in me (and cured by drugs), of my contentious point in life, I hope you will know enough to give me a sufficient amount of subtle liquids, illusory agents, of mental morphine to raise my debasement, to balance what is falling, to rejoin what is disjoined, to recompose what has been destroyed.

My thought salutes you.

PAUL THE BIRDS
or
THE PLACE OF LOVE

Paolo Uccello is struggling amidst a vast mental skein

in which he has lost all the ways of his soul, right down to loss of form, discontinuance of his reality.

Cast away your tongue, Paolo Uccello, cast away your tongue, my tongue, my tongue, dammit, who said that, where are you? Further, further, Mind, Mind, fire, tongues of fire, fire, fire, shut up old goat, shut him up, etc. . . . I rip my tongue out.

YES.

During this time, Brunelleschi and Donatello are tearing themselves apart like the damned. The principal, assayed point under dispute is nevertheless Paolo Uccello, but on another level than them.

There is also Antonin Artaud. But Antonin Artaud in confinement, on the other side of all mental glass, trying as hard as he can to think of himself as elsewhere than there (at André Masson's for instance, who has quite the same appearance as Paolo Uccello, a laminated aspect like an insect or a fool, caught like a fly in the paint, in *his* painting which in consequence becomes laminated).

Besides, Uccello discerns himself in him (Antonin Artaud) but when he discerns himself he is no longer really in him, etc. etc. The fire where his panes steep is transmuted into lovely cloth.

Paolo Uccello continues the ticklish process of this desperate wrenching away of himself.

The problem was raised in Antonin Artaud's mind, but Antonin Artaud does not need problems. He is already troubled enough by his own thoughts, among other things coming face to face with himself and finding himself a bad actor, for instance, yesterday at the cinema in *Surcouf*, without this larva Little Paul coming along to gnaw away at his tongue inside him.

The scenery was planned and put up by him. He has shoved arcades in anywhere and levels on which all the characters strive like dogs.

There is one level for Paolo Uccello, another level for Brunelleschi and Donatello and a little level for Selvaggia, Paolo's wife.

Two or three or even ten problems suddenly criss-cross with their mental tongues zig-zagging and all the interplanetary shifting of their levels.

As the curtain goes up, Selvaggia is dying.

Paolo Uccello enters, asks her how she is. This question has the knack of infuriating Brunelleschi who rips the wholly mental tone of the drama open with a solid clenched fist.

BRUNELLESCHI—Crazy pig.
PAOLO UCCELLO—*Sneezing three times*—Idiot.

First, however, let us describe the characters, give them a physical appearance, a voice and costume.

Paul the Bird's voice is inaudible, he walks like an insect and his robe is too big for him.

Brunelleschi, on the other hand, has a real stage voice, deep and fruity. He looks like Dante.

Donatello is somewhere between the two. St. Francis of Assisi before the Stigmata.

The action takes place on three levels.

No need to tell you Brunelleschi is in love with Paul the Bird's wife. Among other things he blames him for letting her starve to death. Can one starve to death in the Mind?

For we are *solely* in the Mind.

The drama takes place on several levels and has several aspects. It consists as much of the stupid problem of knowing whether Paolo Uccello will muster up enough human compassion to give Selvaggia something to eat, as knowing which of the three or four characters will stay on his own level longest.

For Paolo Uccello represents the Mind, not exactly *pure* but *unconcerned.*

Donatello is Mind exalted. He no longer looks earthwards, although his feet are still on the ground.

Brunelleschi is firmly rooted in this world and he desires Selvaggia in a wordly, sexual way. He thinks of nothing but copulation.

Yet Paolo Uccello is not blind to sex, but he regards it as glazed and mercurial, cold as ether.

As for Donatello, he is past missing it.

Paolo Uccello has nothing under his robe. Just a causeway in place of a heart.

There is a weed at Selvaggia's feet which should not be there.

Brunelleschi suddenly feels his tail swell up and grow enormous. He cannot hold it down and a great white bird flies out of it, like sperm, turning and spiralling in the air.

Dear Sir,

Don't you think it is now time to try and link films with the mind's inmost reality. I am sending you a few extracts from a scenario I sincerely hope you will welcome. You will see its mental design and inner conception give it a place in written language. To make the transition less abrupt, I have prefaced it with two essays which progressively—I mean as they develop—tend to be divided into less and less disinterested imagery.

This scenario was inspired, though only faintly, by what is certainly a poisonous and outworn book. But I am grateful to it, for having led me to discover some of my imagery. And since I am not telling a story, but just disclosing the pictures one by one, you will not be angry with me for only sending you parts of it. Besides, I have two or three pages available for you, where I have made an attempt at Surreality, to make it yield its soul and bring out its wonderful spleen. This could preface the whole and I will send it to you shortly, if you wish.

Yours, etc.

DESCRIPTION OF A PHYSICAL STATE

A sharp, burning sensation in my limbs,

muscles knotted, as if raw, feeling like glass, brittle, fear, cringing at movement or noise. Unconsciously confused steps, gestures and movement. Willpower forever keyed up to make the simplest gestures,

renunciation of simple gestures,

stunning, focal fatigue, a sort of exhausting fatigue. Movements have to be reorganised, a sort of dead tiredness, the mind tired by the exercise of the simplest muscular extension, the act of grasping, unconsciously hanging on to something,

sustained by continuous willpower.

Genetic fatigue, the feeling of dragging one's body about, the feeling of unbelievable fragility becoming splitting pain,

a state of painful numbness, a sort of numbness localised in the skin which does not hinder any movement but changes the sensation within the limbs so that the simple act of standing up straight is achieved only at the cost of a victorious struggle.

Probably localised in the skin, but feeling like the radical removal of a limb and offering the mind nothing but tenuous, woolly pictures of limbs, pictures of distant limbs out of place. A sort of inner breakdown in the entire nervous system.

Variable giddiness, a sort of oblique dazzling accompanies each effort, a thickening heat band gripping the whole surface of my skull, where heat patches detach themselves and move about piece by piece.

Painful inflammation of the skull, gasping nervous tension, the back of the neck doggedly suffering, temples glassy and blotched, head trampled by horses.

Here, we should mention the disembodiment of reality, that sort of break, intent it seems on self-proliferation between objects and the feelings they exercise on our mind, the place they belong.

This instantaneous classification of objects in the brain cells, not so much in their own logical order but in sensed or emotional order,

(which no longer occurs).

Objects now have no smell or gender. But their logical order is also sometimes broken, precisely because it lacks an emotional odour. Words rot at unconscious commands from the brain. All words for no matter what type of mental operation, in particular those which trigger off the mind's most common and active responses.

A slender belly. A belly of fine powder, like a picture. An exploded grenade at the base of the belly.

The grenade casts a fleecy circulation, rising like tongues of fire, cold fire.

The circulation catches the belly, turns it over. Only the belly will not turn.

The veins are full of heady blood, blood mixed with saffron and sulphur, only sulphur sweetened with water.

Breasts appear above the belly. Higher still, and in depth, but on another level of the mind, the sun aflame, only in such a way as to make us think the breast is burning. And at the base of the grenade, a bird.

The sun wears a kind of look. But a look which could look at the sun. This look is conical and upside down on the sun. And all the air is like arrested music, only great, profound music, very solid and secret and full of congealed ramifications.

And the whole is built of columns, a sort of architectural wash-drawing linking the stomach and reality.

The canvas is concave and laminated. The painting is well enclosed in the limits of its canvas. Like a closed circle, a sort of whirling chasm, dividing down the middle. Like a mind which sees and searches through itself, kneaded and endlessly worked over by the mind's clenched hands. Yet the mind sows its phosphorous.

The mind is sure. It really has one foot in this world. The grenade, the belly, the breasts are like proofs testifying to reality. There really is a dead bird, and leafy columns. The air is full of pencil strokes, like knife slashes, like scratches from magic finger nails. The air has been stirred up enough.

And now it sets itself out in cells where the seeds of unreality grow. Fanning out, each cell slips into place.

around the belly, before the sun, beyond the bird and around the circulation of sulphurous water.

But the architecture is indifferent to cells, it nourishes itself and says nothing.

Who knows what germ shines in each egg-bearing cell? In each cell an egg is suddenly born. In each one, a limpid but inhuman teeming goes on, the stratifications of an arrested universe.

Each cell contains its egg properly, offering it to us. But the egg cares little whether it is chosen or rejected.

Not all the cells contain an egg. In some, a spirus is born. And in the air, a larger spirus hangs down as if already sulphurated or even phosphorated and wrapped in unreality. And this spirus is just as important as the most momentous thoughts.

The belly evokes surgery and the Morgue, the factory, public squares and the operating table. The belly's flesh seems made of granite or marble or plaster, only hardened plaster. A slot for a mountain. The sky's spray forms a cool, translucent ring around the mountain. The air around the mountain echoes—pious, legendary and forbidden. Access to the mountain is forbidden. The mountain has its true place in the soul. It is the horizon of something endlessly retreating. It gies one the feeling of an eternal horizon.

As for me, I have described this painting with tears in my eyes, for I am deeply affected by it. I feel my thoughts spread out before it as onto an ideal, ultimate area, only an area whose form could be brought into reality. It is a godsend to me.

And every one of my fibres unravels and finds its place in a predetermined slot. It is as if I were returning to my origins, I sense the location and arrangement of my mind. The person who painted this canvas is the greatest painter in the world. To André Masson, his due.

DARK POET

Dark poet, a maid's breast
Haunts you,
Embittered poet, life seethes
And life burns,
And the sky reabsorbs itself in rain,
Your pen scratches at the heart of life.

Forest, forest, alive with eyes,
On multiple pinions;
With storm-bound hair,
The poets mount horses, dogs.

Eyes fume, tongues stir,
The heavens surge into our senses
Like blue mother's milk;
Women, harsh vinegar hearts,
I hang suspended from your mouths.

LETTER TO THE LEGISLATOR OF THE DRUG ACT

Dear Legislator,

Legislator of the 1916 Bill, passed as the July, 1917 Drug Act, you are an ass.

Your Bill is useless. It only annoys world pharmaceutics without cutting down the nation's drug-taking level.

Because:

(1) The number of drug-addicts who obtain supplies from pharmacies is infinitely small.

(2) Real drug-addicts don't get their supplies from pharmacies.

(3) Drug-addicts who get their supplies from pharmacies are *all* sick.

(4) The number of sick drug-addicts is infinitely small compared with the number of kick-seeking drug-addicts.
(5) Pharmaceutical restrictions on drugs will never bother organised kick-seeking drug-addicts.
(6) There will always be pushers.
(7) There will always be drug-addicts through weakness and desire.
(8) Sick drug-addicts have an inalienable right over society, namely they should be left alone.

The entire problem is a matter of conscience.

The Drug Act turns the right to control a man's suffering over to Public Health inspector-usurpers. This is modern medicine's special claim. It wants to prescribe duty for every man's conscience. All the bleatings of this official charter are powerless to act against this business of consciousness, namely that I am master of my own pain, even more so than death. Every man is the one and only judge of how much physical pain, or again how much mental vacuity, he can honestly stand.

Clearsighted or not, there is an insight no sickness can ever take from me which commands the feelings of my physical life.[1] If I have lost my insight into things, there is

[1] I know only too well that serious personality disturbances can exist and may even lead the conscious self to loss of identity. Consciousness remains intact but no longer recognises itself as its own (and no longer recognises itself at any level).

There are less serious disturbances, or rather to phrase it more correctly, less basic ones, but these are much more painful and more important to the individual and in some ways more *ruinous* to vitality. These occur when consciousness appropriates a whole series of phenomena and really recognises them as its own; phenomena of dislocation, dissolution of its powers during which its materiality is destroyed.

These are just the ones I am alluding to.

But what we must discover is precisely whether life is not more affected by the disembodiment of thought, while retaining an iota of consciousness, than by projecting the conscious into some indefinable elsewhere, while strictly preserving its thought. However it is not a matter of this thought playing us false, or raving, since it is productive, it sheds light, even insane. It happens to exist. And among others, I claim to have no thought.

This makes my friends laugh.

And yet!

For I do not call *having thought*, to judge correctly, I might even say, to *think* correctly. For me, having thought means to *sustain* thought, to be in a fit state to manifest it to oneself and its being able to answer to all circumstances of feeling and life. But mainly *to be answerable to oneself.*

only one thing medicine should do and that is to give me the stuff that allows me to recover the use of this lucidity.

You, Gentlemen, dictators of the French Pharmaceutical College, you are clipped curs. There is one thing you would do better to determine. Which is that opium is the indefeasible, despotic substance that allows those who have had the bad luck to lose life in their souls, to recover it.

There is one sickness against which opium is supreme, this sickness is called Anguish, in its mental, medical, physiological, logical or pharmaceutical form, what you wish.

Anguish which makes men mad.
Anguish which makes men commit suicide.
Anguish which damns men.
Anguish medicine does not know.

For this is where I would place this indefinable and disturbing phenomenon I despair making anyone understand, more particularly my friends (or better still, my enemies, those who take me to be the shadow *I feel I am only too well.* But they do not think to say correctly, shadows twice over, them and me).

I have never seen my friends as I am, their tongues hanging out and their minds terribly checked.

Yes, my thought knows itself, and now despairs ever attaining itself. It knows itself, I mean it suspects itself, in any case it is no longer able to feel itself—I am referring to the physical, material life of thought (and moreover, this is where I am getting back to the subject), I am referring to this modicum of thinking life in a raw state—having not yet reached speech but capable of reaching it when required—without which the soul can no longer live and life is as if it no longer existed. Those who complain of the inadequacy of human thought and their own inability to be satisfied by what they call their thought, confuse and place perfectly differentiated states of mind and form on the same mistaken level, whose lowest is nothing but speech, while the highest is still mind.

If I had what I know to be my thinking mind, I might perhaps have written *Umbilical Limbo*, only I would have written it differently. I have been told I am thinking because I have not completely stopped thinking and because in spite of everything, my mind keeps on a certain plane. It gives proof of its existence from time to time, but no one wants to acknowledge these proofs are weak and lacking interest. But for me, thinking is something else besides being not quite dead, it means being in touch with oneself every moment. It means not to stop feeling oneself within one's inner being for one second, in the unformulated mass of our lives, in the stuff of our real lives. It means not feeling this fundamental chasm, this vital lack in oneself, it means always finding our thinking equal to our thinking, however insufficient the forms we are able to give them may be in other respects. But my own thought, at the same time as sinning by omission, sins also quantitatively. I always think at a lower rate.

Anguish your doctor cannot hear.

Anguish which endangers life.

Anguish which constricts life's umbilical cord.

By your iniquitous Act, you have placed the right to control my anguish, anguish in me as fine as all the needles of all hell's barometers, into the hands of men I have no confidence in whatever; medical asses, dung druggists, malpractising judges, doctors, midwives and grandiloquent inspectors.

Whether the tremors come from the body or the soul, no human seismograph exists which can enable whoever looks to me to assess my pain more exactly than the devastating one in my mind!

All of man's risky knowledge is no greater than the direct knowledge I can have of my own being. I alone can judge what is within me.

Back to your garrets, medical bugs and you too, Legislating Butcher. You do not rant for love of mankind, only because of a tradition of iodicy. Your ignorance of what makes a man is only equalled by your stupidity in restricting him. May your act be visited upon your father, mother, wife, children and all your kind. Now go and stuff your act.

Living acids shake
In hands the poets raise,
On the tables an idolised sky
Stands firm, and a delicate organ

Dips an icy tongue
Into each opening, into each space
Left by the moving sky.

The ground is all shitted up with souls
And women with pretty tufts
Whose tiny little corpses
Uncurl their mummies.

There is an acid, turbid anguish, as sharp as a knife, whose quarterings weigh the earth, flashing anguish, punctuated by abysms, squashed and squeezed like bugs, like a sort of hardened vermin, all movement frozen. Anguish where the mind stifles and cuts itself—killing itself.

It consumes only what belongs to it, it is born of its own asphyxiation.

It is the *coagulation* of the marrow, lack of mental fire, lack of life's circulation.

But opium anguish wears another face, it does not have the same metaphysical bent, or the same marvellously imperfect accentuation. I picture it as full of echoes and vaults, mazes and turnings. Full of talking tongues of fire, of mind's eyes in action and dark thunder filled with reason.

But then I picture the soul as properly centred, yet infinitely divisible and moveable like *an extant object.* I picture it, a sensitive soul, it struggles, yet gives in at the same time, turns its tongues in all directions, multiplies its sex—then kills itself.

You have to know the void as really finespun and organless. Opium's void has a form like a thinking brow which has determined the location of the black pit.

I am talking about the lack of a pit, a sort of cold pictureless suffering, unfeeling, like the indescribable shock of abortions.

THE SPURT OF BLOOD

YOUNG MAN: I love you and everything is fine.

GIRL [*in a quickened, throbbing voice*]: You love me and everything is fine.

YOUNG MAN [*lower*]: I love you and everything is fine.

GIRL [*lower still*]: You love me and everything is fine.

YOUNG MAN [*suddenly turns aside*]: I love you.

Silence.

YOUNG MAN: Face me.

GIRL [*same business, faces him*]: There.

YOUNG MAN [*on an exalted, high-pitched tone*]: I love you, I am great, I am lucid, I am full, I am dense.

GIRL [*same high-pitched tone*]: We love each other.

YOUNG MAN: We are intense. Ah, what a well-made world.

Silence: Noise like a huge wheel spinning, blowing out wind. A hurricane comes between them. At that moment two stars collide, and a succession of limbs of flesh fall. Then feet, hands, scalps, masks, colonnades, porticoes, temples and alembics, falling slower and slower as if through space, then three scorpions one after the other and finally a frog, and a scarab which lands with heart-breaking, nauseating slowness.

YOUNG MAN [*shouting at the top of his voice*]: Heaven's gone crazy.

Looks up at the sky.

Let's run off.

Pushes the GIRL *off ahead of him.*

A Mediaeval KNIGHT *in enormous armour enters, followed by a* WETNURSE *holding her bosom up with her hands and panting because of her swollen breasts.*

KNIGHT: Leave your teats alone. Hand me my papers.

WETNURSE [*giving a shrill cry*]: Oh! Oh! Oh!

KNIGHT: Now what's the matter with you, dammit?

WETNURSE: Our girl there, with him.

KNIGHT: Shush, there's no girl there!

WETNURSE: I tell you they are fucking.

KNIGHT: And what do I care if they are fucking.

WETNURSE: Lecher.

KNIGHT: Balloon.

WETNURSE [*thrusting her hands in pockets as big as her breasts*]: Pimp.

She tosses his papers over hastily.

KNIGHT: Philte, Let me eat.

WETNURSE *runs off. He then gets up and pulls a huge slice of Gruyère cheese out of each paper. He suddenly coughs and chokes.*

KNIGHT [*mouth full*]: Ehp. Ehp. Bring your breasts over here, bring your breasts over here. Where's she gone?

He runs off. YOUNG MAN *returns.*

YOUNG MAN: I saw, I knew, I understood. Here is the main square, the priest, the cobbler, the vegetable stalls, the church portals, the red light, the scales of justice. I can't go on!

A PRIEST, *a* COBBLER, *a* BEADLE, *a* WHORE, *a* JUDGE, *and a* BARROW-WOMAN *advance onto the stage like shadows.*

YOUNG MAN: I have lost her, bring her back.

ALL [*on a different tone*]: Who, who, who, who.

YOUNG MAN: My wife.

BEADLE [*very blustering*]: Your wife, huh, joker!

YOUNG MAN: Joker! She might be yours!

BEADLE [*striking his forehead*]: He could be right!

He runs off.

The PRIEST *steps forward next and puts his arm around the* YOUNG MAN'S *shoulders.*

PRIEST [*as if confessing someone*]: What part of her body did you refer to most often?

YOUNG MAN: To God.

The PRIEST, *disconcerted at this reply, immediately assumes a Swiss accent.*

PRIEST [*with a Swiss accent*]: But that's out of date. We don't look at it in that way. You'll have to ask the volcanoes and earthquakes about that. We gratify ourselves with man's minor indecencies in the confessional. There it is, that's all, that's life.

YOUNG MAN [*very impressed*]: Ah, that's it, that's life! Well, it's a mess.

PRIEST [*still with a Swiss accent*]: Of course.

It suddenly becomes night. The earth quakes. Thunder rages, lightning zig-zagging everywhere and its flashes light up the characters who run about, bump into one another, fall down, get up again and run like mad.

At a given moment a huge hand seizes the WHORE'S *hair which catches fire and swells up visibly.*

A GIGANTIC VOICE: Bitch! Look at your body!

The WHORE'*s body appears completely naked and hideous under her blouse and skirt which turn transparent.*

WHORE: God, let go of me.

She bites God's wrist. A great spurt of blood slashes across the stage, while in the midst of the brightest lightning flash we see the PRIEST *making the sign of the cross.*

When the lights come up again, the characters are all dead and their corpses lie all over the ground. Only the WHORE *and* YOUNG MAN *are left, devouring each other with their eyes.*

The WHORE *falls into the* YOUNG MAN'*s arms.*

WHORE [*with a sigh, as if in an orgiastic climax*]: Tell me how it happened.

The YOUNG MAN *hides his head in his hands.*

The WETNURSE *returns carrying the* GIRL *under her arms like a parcel.*

The GIRL *is dead. She drops her on the ground where she sprawls out and becomes as flat as a pancake.*

The WETNURSE'*s breasts are gone. Her chest is completely flat.*

At that moment, the KNIGHT *enters and throws himself on the* WETNURSE, *shaking her violently.*

KNIGHT [*in a terrible voice*]: Where did you put it? Give me my Gruyère.

WETNURSE [*brazenly*]: Here!

She lifts up her dress.

The YOUNG MAN *wants to run off but he freezes like a paralysed puppet.*

YOUNG MAN [*in a ventriloquist's voice and as if hovering in mid-air*]: Don't hurt Mummy.

KNIGHT: Damn her.

He hides his face in horror.

A host of scorpions crawl out from under the WETNURSE'*s dress and start swarming in her vagina which swells and splits, becomes transparent and shimmers like the sun.*

The YOUNG MAN *and* WHORE *fly off like mad.*

GIRL [*gets up, dazzled*]: The Virgin! Ah, that's what he was looking for.

CURTAIN

NERVE SCALES

NERVE SCALES

I really felt you break down the environment around me, I felt you create a void to allow me to progress, making room for an impossible space, for what was then only potentiality within me. For an entire, virtual germination yet to come, drawn into the spot that presented itself.

I have often got myself into this impossible, absurd state, so as to try and create thought within me. There are a few of us in these times, who want to cut things down and so create areas for life within us, areas which did not exist and did not seem to belong in space.

I have always been struck by the mind's obstinacy in wanting to think in terms of measurement or areas, in fastening on arbitrary states of things so as to think. Thinking in segments, in crystalloids, so that each form of existence remains fixed in the beginning and thought does not communicate with objects instantaneously and uninterrupted. But this fixation, this immobilisation, this sort of monumentalisation of the soul occurs BEFORE THOUGHT, so to speak. Obviously these are the right conditions for creativity.

But I am even more struck by those unrelenting, meteoric illusions which send us predetermined, limited, planned constructions, those clear-cut segments of the soul, as if they were a great plastic page, porous to the rest of reality. Surreality is like a sort of osmotic contraction, a sort of inverted communication. Far from seeing any weakening in control, on the contrary control seems to me more assured, but control which instead of acting remains on guard and prevents contact with day to day reality and allows more subtle and rarified contacts,

contacts reduced to a thread which catches fire but never breaks.

I picture a soul, worn down and as if changed into brimstone and phosphorous by these contacts, as the only acceptable state of reality.

But I do not know what unknown, unnameable clear-sightedness furnishes me with their tone and sound and makes me feel them myself. I feel them as a certain insoluble whole, I mean doubt never affects this feeling. As for me, in relation to these disturbing contacts, I am in a state of almost complete immobility. You might look on it as an arrested void, a mental mass buried somewhere, become virtuality.

An actor, seen as through crystal.
Inspiration in stages.
Literature must not show too much.

I have only aimed at the mechanism of the soul, I have only transcribed the pain of abortive adjustments.

I am really abysmal. Those who believed me capable of consummate suffering, great suffering, sustained, fulsome anguish, anguish which is a mixture of different things, an excited grinding of powers and not a suspended point

—yet with lively, uprooting impulses, stemming from the confrontation of my powers with these proffered supreme depths,

(the confrontation of great and mighty powers)

there is nothing now but unfathomable depths, cold, a halt,

—thus those who attributed more life to me, who did not think me so far fallen within myself, who believed me submerged in agonizing noise, violent darkness against which I struggled,

—are lost in the shades of man.

In sleep, my nerves are taut down my legs.

Sleep came from the shifting of belief, the tension relaxed and absurdity irked me.

We must understand intelligence is only an enormous contingency, we may lose it, not like a dead madman, but as a person living in life, who feels its pull and inspiration (not of life, that is, but intelligence).

The titillations of intelligence and this brusque reversing of roles.

Words half-way to intelligence.

The faculty of hindsight, or suddenly railing against our thoughts.

This dialogue in thought.

Absorbed, breaking off everything.

Then suddenly this trickle of water on a volcano, the mind's slight, slow slip.

Finding oneself in a state of extreme shock, enlightened by unreality, with fragments of the real world in a corner of oneself.

To think with the minimum of discontinuity, without any traps in our thought, without one of those sudden disappearing tricks my bones are accustomed to as energy transmitters.

At times my bones take pleasure in these games, delight in these games, delight in these stealthy abductions presided over by my mind, my head.

At times I am only at a loss for one word, a simple unimportant little word, to be great, to speak in the tone of the prophets. A corroborating word, an exact word, a subtle word, a word thoroughly steeped in my bones, come out of me to stand at the furthest limits of my being, and which would be nothing to most men.

I am the witness, the only witness of my self. This covering of words, those imperceptible whispered changes of thought, this smallest particle of my thought which I assert was already expressed yet which miscarried.

I am the only judge in gauging their scope.

A sort of continuous wasting of the normal level of reality.

Inside this crust of skin and bone which is my head there is a constant anguish, not like having a moral dilemma, or like the thought processes of those ridiculously fussy natures whose worries, like leaven, are continually rising to the top, but like a (decantation)

within

like the dispossession of my vital substance

like the physical and essential loss

(I mean loss of essence)

of a sense.

A powerlessness to fix unconsciously the point of rupture of automatism at any level whatsoever.

The difficult part is to find out exactly where one is, to re-establish communication with one's self. The whole thing lies in a certain flocculation of objects, the gathering of these mental gems about one as yet undiscovered nucleus.

Here, then, is what I think of thought:

INSPIRATION CERTAINLY EXISTS.

And there is a luminous point where all reality is rediscovered, only changed, transformed, by—what?—a nucleus of the magic use of things. And I believe in mental meteorites, in personal cosmogonies.

Do you know what suspended sensitivity is, this sort of tremendous vitality split in two. This necessary, cohesive point to which being no longer rises, this menacing, crushing place.

Dear Friends,

What you took to be my works were only my waste matter, those soul scrapings a normal man does not welcome.

Since then, my problem has not been whether my disorders got better or worse, but rather my mind's persistant pain and apoplexy.

Here I am back in M . . . , where I have felt sensations of sluggishness and dizziness again, a sudden terrible craving for sleep, a sudden loss of strength accompanied by a feeling of great pain, of headlong degradation.

Here is someone in whom no part of his mind congeals, who does not suddenly feel his soul is on the left, on the heart side. Here is someone for whom life is a focal point and for whom the soul has no sides, nor the mind any beginnings.

I am stupid because I suppress my thoughts, because my thoughts are ill-formed. I am empty for I am stupefied by speech.

A certain number of ill-formed, ill-accumulated vitreous corpuscles you use so thoughtlessly. You know nothing about this use, having never watched it.

All the terms I choose to think with are TERMS for me in the proper sense of the word, true endings, bordering my mental (   )[1] and all the states of mind to which I have subjected my thoughts. I am truly LOCALISED by my terms and if I say I am LOCALISED by my terms, it means I do not acknowledge them as valid in my thought. I am really paralysed by my terms, by a succession of endings. And WHEREVER my thoughts may be at such times, I can only bring them out through these terms, however contradictory to it, lateral or equivocal they may be, or pay the penalty and stop thinking at such times.

If only we could enjoy our void, if we could be properly relaxed in our void, if this void were not some sort of being, but not quite death either.

It is so hard no longer to exist, no longer to be in something. Real pain is to feel thought shift within us. But when thought has a point, it is surely not suffering.

[1] Word missing.

I have reached the point where I am no longer in contact with life, yet within me I have all the urges and insistent titillations of being. I now only have one task, to make myself.

I lack the coordination of my speech with the moment of my moods.

"Well, that's normal, everyone is at a loss for words at times, you are too hard on yourself to hear you one would never think so, you express yourself perfectly well in French, you attach too much importance to words."

You are asses, from the brainiest to the lightweights, from the sharpest to the thickest, you are asses, I mean you are sons-of-bitches, I mean you yap about outside, you rabidly persist in not understanding. I know myself and that is enough for me. It must be enough. I know myself because I am watching myself, I am observing Antonin Artaud.

—You may know yourself, but we see you. We can perfectly well see what you are up to.

—Yes, but you cannot see my thoughts.

There are gaps and stops at every stage in my thinking mechanism. Understand me clearly, I do not mean in time, I mean in a certain sort of space (I understand myself). I do not mean thought which is spun out, thought measured in length of thought. I mean one thought, only one, an INNER thought. But I do not mean one of Pascal's concepts, philosophic concepts, I mean a warped fixation, the sclerosis of a particular condition. Take that!

I am studying myself microscopically. I indicate the fault's, the unadmitted landslide's, exact spot. For the mind is more reptilian than you, Gentlemen, it slips away snake-like, it slips away until it jeopardises our speech, I mean it leaves it in suspense.

I am the man who has most felt the stupefying confusion of his language in relation to thought. I am the man who has best charted his inmost self, and its most imperceptible subsidences. I truly lose myself in thought like in dreams, the way one returns to thought, suddenly. I am he who knows the inmost recesses of loss.

Writing is all trash.

People who leave the realm of the obscure in order to define whatever is going on in their minds, are trash.

The whole pack of literati are trash, particularly these days.

All those who fix landmarks in their minds, I mean in a certain part of their heads, in strictly localised areas of their brains, all those who are masters of their own language, all those for whom words mean something, all those for whom there are currents of thought and who think the soul can be sublime; those who are the spirit of the times, and who have named these currents of thought I am thinking of their specific tasks and the mechanical creaking their minds give out at every gust of wind,

—are trash.

Those for whom certain words and modes of being have only one meaning, those who are so fussy, those who classify feelings and who quibble over some degree or other of their laughable classifications, those who still believe in "terms" those who stir the ideological pots that are in vogue at the time, those about whom women speak so well and the same women who speak so well and speak about contemporary currents of thought, those who still believe in orientation of the mind, those who follow paths, who drop names, who have pages of books acclaimed,

—those are the worst trash.

You are very free, young man!

No, I am thinking of bearded critics.

I told you; no works, no language, no words, no mind, nothing.

Nothing, except fine Nerve Scales.

A sort of impenetrable stop in the midst of everything in our minds.

Do not expect me to tell you what all this is called or into how many sections it is divided, or to tell you its value. Or that I will be had on, so that I will begin to discuss all this and, in discussing it, will become confused and in so doing, will, without realising it, start THINKING. Or clarify it, or bring it to life, to adorn it with a host of words, polished meanings, all different and clearly able to bring to light all the attitudes and shades of very sensitive and penetrating thought.

Ah, these unnamed states, these superior positions of the soul, Ah, these periods in the mind, Ah, these tiny failures which are the stuff of my days, Ah, these masses teeming with facts. Still, I use the same words and yet my thoughts don't appear to advance much, but really I am advancing more than you, bearded asses, apposite swine, masters of the false word, despatchers of portraits, gutter writers, graziers, entomologists and scabs on my tongue.

I told you my speech no longer existed, but this is no reason for you to persist, for you obstinately to go on speaking.

Come now, in ten years' time I will be understood by people who do what you are doing today. Then my eruptions will be understood, my crystals will be clear, they will have learnt how to adulterate my poisons and the play of my soul will be divulged.

By then all my hair, all my mental veins will be melted in quicklime, then my bestiary will be noted and my mystique will have become a cover. Then the joints in the stones will appear, fuming, and arboreal bunches of mind's eyes will set into glossaries and stone aeroliths will fall. Then lines will appear, then non-spatial geometry will be understood and people will learn what the configuration of mind means and they will understand how I lost my mind.

Then you will understand why my mind is not here, then you will see all language exhausted, all minds dry up, all tongues shrivel up, all human figures will collapse, will deflate, as if drawn up by shrivelling leeches. And this-lubrifying membrane will go on floating in the air, this lubrifying, caustic membrane, this doubly-thick membrane, multi-levelled, infinitely fissured, this sad, translucent membrane. Yet it, too, so sensitive, so relevant, so capable of multiplying, splitting, turning inside out, with its shimmering fissures, senses, drugs and its penetrating, noxious irrigation.

Then all this will be considered all right.

And I will have no further need to speak.

DOMESTIC LETTER

Each one of your letters outdoes the last in lack of understanding and narrowness of mind. Like all women, you make judgements with your body, not your mind. You must be joking if you think your justifying yourself upset me! What did enrage me was when one of my explanations led you to resort to arguments you considered had obviously quashed mine.

All your reasons and endless arguments will never add up to your knowing anything about my life or to judge me on the very smallest part of it. I would not even need to justify myself to you, if you yourself were a reasonable, well-balanced woman, but you get carried away by your imagination, by your over-acute sensitivity which prevents you from seeing the truth when confronted by it. It is impossible to discuss anything with you. I have only one more thing to say to you. My mind has always been just as confused, my body and soul just as prostrate, my nerves just as though constricted for either longer or shorter intervals. If you had seen me a few years ago, before I could even have been suspected of the habit you reproach me for, you would not be surprised now at the reappearance of these phenomena. Besides, if you are convinced, if you feel their reappearance is due to that, there is obviously nothing more to say, one can't fight feelings.

At all events, I can no longer count on you in my distress since you refuse to show any concern for the most affected part of me, my soul. Besides, just like all women, like fools, you have never judged me on anything except outward appearances while my inner soul is the most shattered and broken part of me. I cannot forgive you for that, as unfortunately for me, the two do not always coincide. And furthermore, I forbid you to bring the subject up again.

SECOND DOMESTIC LETTER

I need a simple, well-balanced woman beside me, not one whose worried, troubled, soul eternally nourishes my despair. I never saw you of late without a feeling of fear and uneasiness. I am fully aware your love makes you worry about me, but it is your soul, sick and unnatural like mine, which intensifies your worries and causes you to fret. I don't want to live near you in fear any more.

I might add, I need a woman who belongs solely to me and whom I can find at home any hour of the day. I am desperately lonely. I can no longer go home in the evenings to my room, alone, without some creature comforts about me. I need a home, I need one right away and a woman who cares for me all the time, and who looks after me in every little way, since I am incapable of looking after anything. An artist like you has your own life to lead and cannot do that. Everything I am saying is brutally selfish, but it is so. This woman would not even have to be very pretty, I don't want her to be outstandingly intelligent either, and above all she shouldn't brood too much. It would be enough if she were attached to me.

I think you can appreciate how very frank I am in speaking to you like this and you will show your intelligence by the following. You must understand everything I say has nothing to do with the fervent tenderness, the inalienable love I feel and will irrevocably feel for you, but this feeling itself has nothing to do with normal, everyday life. Life is there to be lived. There are too many things which bind me to you to ask you to break things off. I am only asking you to change our relationship, to allow each of us a different life, yet in such a way that we shall not be estranged.

THIRD DOMESTIC LETTER

I have stopped existing for five days now, because of you, because of your stupid letters, your irrational, physical letters, your letters full of physical reactions, without conscious reasoning. My nerves are frayed, I am at the end of my tether. Instead of humouring me, you abuse me. You abuse me because what you say is not true. You have never been right, you always judged me with the basest feminine sensitivity. You refuse to take to any of my arguments. As for me, I have no further reasons to give, no more excuses to make, I am not going to argue with you. I know my life, that's enough. The moment I am beginning to find my feet, you progressively sap my strength and make me despair again. The more I give you reason to hope, to be patient, to stand me, the less you condone my faults, the more you are bent on harrying me, causing me to lose the advantages of my gains. You know nothing of the mind or its disorders. You judge everything by externals. But I know my own inner self, don't I, and when I cry out that there is nothing within me, nothing in my personality that is not caused by the existence of a disorder which comes before my ego, before my will, nothing in any of my vilest reactions that does not come solely from my disorder and which, whatever the case may be, cannot but be attributed to it, yet you fall back on one of your wretched rationalisations. You start to churn out the wrong reasons which you tack on to some trifling details about me, which make judgements on me from the pettiest side. Whatever I may have done with my life, however, has not stopped me slowly moving into my being again and feeling a little more at home there each day. Into this being my disorder robbed me of and which the ebb and flow of life has restored in me bit by bit. If you did not know what I had devoted myself to, in order to restrain or remove the agony of that unbearable separation, you would stand my lack of balance, my shocks, my unstable moods, the crumbling of my physical being, my abstraction and states of collapse. You heap abuse on me, you threaten me, you drive me into a panic, your angry fingers even ransack my brain's grey matter, because you suppose the above are due to my using a substance, the very thought of which makes you lose your senses. Yes, you make me conflict with myself, each of your letters makes me of two minds, throws me into insane dead-locks and riddles me with despair or fury. I cannot go on. I beg you to stop. Stop thinking with your body, take life in once and for all, all of life. Welcome life, think things over, think of me, give in and give life a chance to let me alone a bit, let it slacken off in me, before me. Stop abusing me. Enough.

The Grid is a terrible moment for sensitivity and substance.

FRAGMENTS FROM A DIARY IN HELL

to André Gaillard

Neither my cry nor my fever are mine. Can you imagine just how tenacious my secondary faculties, those hidden elements of mind and soul, must be, even in their state of disintegration.

This thing, half-way between the tenor of my typical mood and the head of my reality.

I am not so much in need of nourishment as a sort of basic consciousness.

This vital centre in life which the emanations of thought cling to.

A stifling, vital centre.

Simply to settle on some clear truth, that is to say one with only one edge.

This problem, the emaciation of my ego, no longer appears solely from a painful aspect. I feel there are new factors intervening in perverting my life and I have a sort of new consciousness of my intimate weakening.

I see my whole reason for being alive in the act of throwing the dice, throwing myself into the assertion of intuitively-felt truths, however chancy they may be.

I linger for hours over the impression an idea or sound has made on me. My emotion does not develop in time or have any temporal sequence. The ebb and flow of my soul is in perfect harmony with the absolute idealisation of my mind.

To confront the metaphysics I created for myself, in accordance with the void I carry within me.

This suffering is driven into me like a wedge, in the centre of my purest reality, at the spot in sensibility where the two worlds, mind and body, meet. I have learnt to take my mind off it by the effect of a false suggestion.

In the momentary space a lie's illusion lasts, I concoct a notion of escape, I rush off on a false track prompted by my blood. I close my intellectual eyes, allowing the unformulated to speak within me, I give myself the illusion of a system whose terminology escapes me. But from this mistaken moment, the feeling lingers that I have snatched something real from the unknown. I believe in spontaneous spells. On the paths along which my blood takes me, I cannot help discovering one truth some day.

Paralysis overcomes me, progressively stops me finding my feet, I no longer have any support, any base.

I seek myself anywhere. My thoughts can no longer go where the emotions and imagery that arise in me lead them. I feel emasculated right down to my slightest impulses. I have ended up seeing right through me, as a result of the utter renunciation of my intellect and emotion. I must make it understood; what is really affected in me is the living man, and this stifling paralysis is the centre of my usual personality and not of my feeling a predestined being. I am definitely apart from life. My torment is as ingenious and devilish as it is harsh. I have to exert my imagination wildly, tenfold, because of the grip of this stifling asphyxiation, to succeed in *discovering* what my sickness is. And if I persist in this pursuit, needing to settle the state of my suffocation once and for all. . . .

You were certainly wrong to mention this paralysis which threatens me. In fact it does threaten me and gains on me every day. It already exists as a horrible reality. I still have control over my limbs (though for how long?) but it has been a long time since I had any control over my mind, and my entire unconscious dictates to me with impulses which come from the depths of my nervous frenzy and swirling blood. Quick, hurried images which to my mind spell out only angry words and blind hate, yet which are over as quick as a knife thrust or lightning in a congested sky.

I am branded by an urgent death in which death itself holds no terrors for me.

I feel the despair brought by these terrifying forms advancing on me, is alive. It slips into this living vital centre beyond which the paths of eternity extend. It is truly eternal separation. It slips its knives into that focus where I feel myself human. It severs the vital cords which link me with the dreams of my own clear reality.

Forms of capital despair (truly vital),
Crossroads of separation,

Crossroads of awareness of my flesh,
Abandoned by my body,
Abandoned by every possible human feeling.

I can only compare it to that condition in the throes of a delirious fever during a serious illness.

I am dying of the torment created by this paradox between my inner facility and my external difficulty.

Time may pass and the world's social upheavals may play havoc with the thought of man. I am safe from all thought steeped in phenomena. Leave me to my dark clouds, my eternal unproductivity, to my irrational hopes. But let it be quite clear I renounce none of my errors. If I judge incorrectly my flesh is at fault, only these lights my mind permits to filter through hourly are my flesh, its blood clothed in lightning.

He spoke to me about Narcissism. I retorted it was my life. I do not worship my ego but the flesh, the word flesh in its sensed meaning. Things concern me only in so far as they affect my flesh and coincide with it at the very point they arouse it, but not beyond it. Nothing concerns or interests me save what is addressed *directly* to my flesh. Now he is talking about the Self. I retort Ego and Self are two distinct terms that are not to be confused and are precisely the two terms which balance each other and maintain the body's equilibrium.

I feel the ground crumbling under my thought, I am forced to consider the terms I use, unsupported by their inner meaning, or individual substratum. And more than that, the point where this substratum seemed to connect with my life suddenly grows strangely perceptible and virtual to me. I have the impression of an unforseen and fixed space where normally all is movement, communication, interference and travel.

But this erosion which strikes at the basis of my thoughts, in its most urgent communications with the intellect and the mind's intuitive spirit, does not take place in an abstract, unfeeling realm where only the highest areas of the brain would participate. More than the mind, which remains unharmed, though encircled with barbs, this erosion strikes and diverts thought's nervous travel. These lacunae and stoppages are especially felt in the limbs and blood.

Extreme cold.

Agonizing abstinence.

Bone and sinew nightmare limbo, with a sensation of my gastric functions flapping like a flag in the corposant of the storm.

Unformed images to be prodded as if with a finger, but not related to any substance of any kind.

I am a man by virtue of my hands and feet, my belly, my heart of flesh and blood, my stomach whose knots unite me with life's decomposition.

People mention words, but this has nothing to do with words, the mind's duration is being called into question.

We must not suppose the soul is not implicated in this falling word-shell. Life and the mind go side by side there is a human being in the circle the mind revolves upon, linked to it by a multitude of fibres. . . .

No, all the physical rendings, all the curtailment in physical activity and the discomfort at feeling dependent within our body, and this body itself laden with stone and resting on decayed supports, are not as bad as the affliction in being deprived of physical knowledge and one's sense of inner balance. When the soul lacks language or language fails the mind and this cleavage breaks open a great furrow of despair and blood in the sensory field, this is the great affliction which undermines not the shell or frame but the MATERIAL of the body. We must lose this erratic sense of excitement which we feel has been a trap enclosing the world to its fullest extent, and we must lose this feeling of futility such as it is, which is like the cold hand of death. This futility is as it were the mental colour of the trap and of that intense stupefaction, while its physical colour is the taste of blood issuing in spurts through the orifices of the brain.

It is no good telling me this death-trap is inside me. I am part of life, I represent the fate which has chosen me and it is impossible all earthly life would include me in with it at a given moment, since it threatens the principle of life by its very nature.

Something exists over and above all human activity; this is the example of the monotonous crucifixion, this crucifixion where the soul is unendingly lost.

That cord connecting me with the intellect which preoccupies me and the subconscious which nourishes me, reveals more and more subtle fibres at the heart of its tree-like tissue. And this is a new life, born, forever more profound, expressive and firmly rooted.

This choking soul will never give any precise details because the torture which is killing it, stripping it fibre by fibre, occurs beneath thought, beneath what speech may express, since it is the liaison itself of what makes it and holds it spiritually bound together, which breaks down progressively as life summons it to continuous clarity. Never any daylight shed on this suffering, on this sort of cyclical, fundamental martyrdom. Yet it lives, though suffering continual eclipses, when the fleeting is constantly intermingled with the fixed, and the confused with the penetrating language of short-lived daylight. This curse is highly instructive to the depths it inhabits, but the world will not learn its lesson.

The emotions engendered by the blossoming of a form, adapting my humours to the virtuality of short speech, is a condition differently dear to me than sating my activity.

It is the touchstone of certain spiritual lies.

This sort of backwards step the mind takes short of consciousness staring it in the face, to go in search of the emotion of being alive. The entire soul flows, passes into the intense heat of that emotion, situated outside the particular spot where the mind looked for it, which emerges with its richly dense, freshly cast forms, that emotion which renders the bewildering sound of matter to the mind. What delights the soul more than fire is the limpidity, the ease, the natural glacial candour of this overly fresh substance, blowing hot and cold.

Here is a man who knows what the appearance of this substance means and what its blossoming forth costs in subterranean massacres. This substance is the standard of a void which does not know itself.

When I am trying to discover myself, my thoughts seek one another in the regions of new space. I am up in the moon, dreaming, while others sit at home. I partake in planetary gravitation within the fissures of my mind.

Life will continually develop, events will take place, spiritual conflicts will be resolved but I will not share in them. I can expect nothing either on the moral or physical side. Continual pain and darkness are my lot, night in my soul, and I have no voice to cry out.

Squander your riches far from this unfeeling body, unaffected by any mental or spiritual seasons.

I have chosen the realm of pain and darkness, just as others chose radiance and amassing substance.

I do not labour in any area, in any field.

I only labour in eternity.

ART AND DEATH

WHO, IN THE HEART ...

Who, in the heart of some anxiety at the bottom of certain dreams, has not known death as a marvellous, disruptive feeling which could never be confused with anything else of a mental order? One must have experienced this exhausting crescendo of anguish which comes over one in waves and then swells one up as if forced by some unbearable bellows. Anguish which draws near then withdraws, each time stronger, more ponderous and replete. This is the body itself, having reached the limit of its strength and distension, and yet must go on. It is a sort of suction cup on the soul, whose acridity spreads like acid into the furthermost bounds of the senses. And the soul cannot even fall back on a breakdown. For this distension itself is false. Death is not so easily satisfied. In the order of physical experience, this distension is like an inverted image of the contraction which takes possession of the mind *over the whole extent of the living body.*

This held-in gasp is the last, really the last. It is time for taking stock. The moment we have feared, dreaded and dreamt about so much has arrived. One is going to die, this is true. One watches and measures one's breath. And time unfurls completely, in all its intensity, and is resolved in such a way it is bound to dissolve without a trace.

Die, dogged bone. They are well aware your thought is not complete or finished and whatever way you turn you have not even *started* thinking.

Little matter. The fear that battens down on you is drawing and quartering you in exact proportion to this impossibility. For you well know we must cross to the other side and nothing in you is prepared for this, not even this body, especially this body you will take leave of without ever forgetting its substance, density or impossible asphixia.

And it will be just like a bad dream where you are outside the position of your body, having none the less dragged it this far, making you suffer, and enlightening you with its deafening impressions. Where the perspective is always larger or smaller than you, where none of the feeling of ancient earthly orientation you bear can be satisfied any longer.

That is it, that is it forever. What is this cry, like a dog howling in a dream, which makes your skin crawl, gives you this feeling of grief and unnameable uneasiness making you gag in a mad drowning frenzy. No, it isn't true. It isn't true.

But the worst of it is, it is true. And at the same time there is this feeling of desperate truth, where it seems you are going to die again, you are going to die a second time. (You say to yourself, you say the words, you are going to die. You are going to die. *I am going to die a second time.*)—At that moment some humidity, some moisture from iron or rock or wind refreshes you unbelievably and eases your mind, and you yourself liquify, you get used to flowing in to death, your new state of death. This running water is death and from the moment when you contemplate yourself serenely and register your new sensations, it means the great identification has begun. You died, yet here you are alive again.—ONLY THIS TIME YOU ARE ALONE.

I have just described a sensation of anguish and dreams, anguish worming its way into dreams and this is more or less how I imagine agony worms its way into you and finally ends in death.

In any case, such dreams cannot lie. They do not lie. And these sensations of death laid out end to end, this stifling, this despair, drowsiness, desolation, and silence, don't we see them enlarged in a dream and suspended with the feeling that one of the facets of a new reality is forever looking over our shoulder?

But in the depths of death or dreams, anguish begins anew. This anguish, stretched like a rubber-band that suddenly snaps at your throat, is neither new nor unknown. Death you slipped into unaware, your body rolling back into a ball, this head—it had to pass through, containing life and consciousness as it did, and consequently supreme suffocation, and consequently the greater dismemberment—it, too, had to pass through the smallest possible opening. But it is anguished to the limit of its pores and this head, by dint of shaking and turning fearfully has an inkling, the feeling it is swollen and its terror has assumed a shape and broken out in pimples under the skin.

And as there is nothing new about death after all, on the contrary it is only too well known, for at the end of this visceral distillation don't we picture the panic we have already experienced? It seems the fierceness of this despair revives certain childhood situations when death appeared so clearly, like uninterrupted chaos. Childhood knows sudden awakenings of the mind, intense prolongations of thought we lose again as we grow older. Death incontestably appears in certain childhood panic-stricken fears, in a certain spectacular, irrational terror where a feeling of extra-human threats lurks.

Like the rending of a membrane near at hand, like the lifting of a veil which is the world—still unformed and unsafe.

Who has no memory of extraordinary enlargements of a wholly mentally real order, which did not amaze us at the time and which were given, truly delivered to the wilderness of our childhood senses? These extensions were impregnated with perfect knowledge, pervading everything, crystal-clear and eternal.

But what strange thoughts it emphasises, from what disintegrated meteorite does it reconstitute human atoms.

The child sees recognisable throngs of ancestors in which he notes the origins of all known man-to-man likenesses. The world of appearance swells and overflows into the imperceptible and the unknown. But an overshadowing of life occurs and henceforth such states never recur unless graced with the help of wholly abnormal clearsight due, for example, to drugs.

Hence the immense usefulness of these narcotics to free

and heighten the mind. True or false from the standpoint of a reality we have seen we could set small store by, this reality being only one of the most transitory and least recognisable facets of infinite reality, this reality being the same as matter and decaying with it and from a mental standpoint narcotics regain their higher dignity which makes them the closest and most useful aids to death.[1]

This death bound hand and foot, wherein the soul writhes in trying finally to regain a complete, porous state,

where everything is not shock, nor the jagged edges, the delirious confusion of endless rationalisations, mingling in the fibres of a simultaneously unbearable and harmonious jumble,

where everything is not sickness,

where the smallest place is not ceaselessly reserved for the greatest hunger, hungering after unrestricted space which would be definitive this time,

[1] I affirm—and stick to the idea that death is not outside the field of the mind and that, within certain limitations, is knowable and approachable by a certain sensibility.

Everything in the order of the written word which abandons the field of clear, orderly perception, everything which aims at reversing appearances and introduces doubt about the position of mental images and their relationship to one another, everything which provokes confusion without destroying the strength of our emergent thought, everything which disrupts the relationship between things by giving this agitated thought an even greater aspect of truth and violence—all these offer death a loophole and put us in touch with certain more acute states of mind in the throes of which death expresses itself.

This is why all those who dream without regretting their dreams, without bringing back this feeling of atrocious nostalgia after diving down into the fertile unconscious, are swine. A dream is the truth. All dreams are true. I have a feeling of harshness, of landscapes as if sculpted, pieces of wavy ground covered with a sort of cool sand which means:

"Regret, disappointment, abandonment, separation, when will we meet again?"

Nothing resembles love so much as the appeal of certain dream landscapes, the encirclement of certain hills by a clay-like material whose forms seem moulded onto our thoughts.

When will we meet again? When will the earthy taste of your lips return again to touch my anxious mind? The earth is like some kind of whirlwind of mortal lips. Before us, life scoops out a pit of all our missed caresses. What must we do with this angel at our side, whose apparition never happened? Will all our sensations forever be intellectual and will our dreams never succeed in kindling a soul whose feelings will help us die. What is this death where we are alone forever, where love never shows us the way?

where this paroxysmal pressure suddenly breaks through the feeling of a new level,

where from the depths of a nameless jumble this writhing, snorting soul feels able, as in dreams, to become awakened to a clearer world and after having bored through it knows not what barrier—finds itself in luminosity where it stretches its limbs at last and where the world's partitions seem infinitely fragile.

This soul could be reborn, however it is not reborn. For although eased, it still feels it is dreaming, it still has not transformed itself into that dream state with which it is unable to identify.

At this instant in his mortal daydream, living man arrives before the great wall of impossible identification and brutally withdraws his soul.

He is then thrown back onto the naked level of his senses, in groundless light.

Outside the infinite musicality of nerve waves, a prey to the boundless hunger of the air, to absolute cold.

LETTER TO THE CLAIRVOYANTE

For André Breton

Madam,

You live in a poor room in the midst of life. We would like to hear the sky murmur at your windows, but in vain. Nothing, neither your appearance, nor an air distinguishes you from us, but some foolishness or other more deeply-rooted than experience leads us to endlessly slash and banish your face, right down to the jointures of your life.

You know when I sit before you with a torn, sullied soul, I am only a shadow, but I am not afraid of this terrible knowledge. I know you are in all my vital centres and much closer to me than my mother. It is as if I were naked before you. Naked, unchaste and naked, upright, like a ghost of myself, but unashamed, for in your eyes running dizziliy through my sinews, evil is really sinless.

I have never found I was so precise, so concentrated, so self-assured even above scruple and beyond all spite, whether that of others or my own and also so discerning. You added a fire tip, a stellar tip to the quivering thread of my hesitation. Neither judged, nor judging *myself*, effortlessly whole, unstrivingly complete. Except for life, it was bliss. And at last no more fear my tongue, my over-thick tongue, my minute tongue would fork. I hardly needed to bestir my thoughts.

I entered your place, meanwhile, without terror or a trace of the most normal curiosity. And yet you were the mistress, the oracle, and you could have seemed to me the very soul and God of my horrible destiny. Able to see and tell me! That nothing unclean or secret is obscured, but everything buried comes to light, at last the repressed spreads itself out before this absolutely pure judge's fine panoramic eye. One who discerns and disposes but who does not even know she can crush you.

The perfect, soft light where our souls no longer make us suffer and yet they are infested with evil. Light without cruelty or passion, where only one mood is revealed, a mood of serene, pious, rare fatalism. Yes, visiting you Madam, I was no longer afraid of dying. In life or in death, I saw nothing but a great peaceful expanse where the shades of my destiny melted away. I was really safe, free from all trouble, for even my future trouble was sweet to me, as if there were *the remotest chance* I could ever have any trouble to fear in the future.

My destiny was no longer this covered way concealing only evil beneath it. I had lived eternally dreading it, and, *though remote*, I felt it close by and ever submerged within me. No violent eddies upset my nerves in advance, I had already been too stricken and upset by misfortune. My nerves now recorded only a huge, soft, uniform mass. I didn't much care if the most terrible doors opened before me, the terrors were already behind me. And the impending future, although bad, only affected me as harmonious discord, a series of peaks reversed, turned in on themselves and blunted within me. You, Madam, could only foretell my life growing smoother.

But what reassured me above all was not this deep certainty, physically wedded to me, but really the feeling of the uniformity of all things. The Splendid Absolute. No doubt I had learnt to reconcile myself to death, which is why all things, even the most cruel, now only seemed to me to appear balanced, their meaning being perfectly immaterial.

Yet there was something more. Though I was unconcerned about this meaning and its direct effect on my person, it was still imbued with something good. I approached you entirely optimistically. This optimism did not stem from an inclination of the mind but from the deep knowledge of the equilibrium in which my whole life was bathed. My life to come, balanced by my terrible past, which painlessly entered death; I *knew* of my death beforehand like the consummation of life, smooth at last and sweeter than my finest memories. And reality grew visibly, and developed into that supreme knowledge where the value of present life begins to fall apart under the hammers of eternity. Eternity could now not help revenging me for the desperate sacrifice of my self in which I took no part. My immediate future, my future starting from the moment when I entered your circle for the first time, this future also belonged to death. And you, your appearance was favourable to me from the first.

My emotion at knowing this was dominated by being conscious of the infinite meekness of existence.[1] For me,

[1] I cannot help it. I felt like this in front of Her. Life was good because this clairvoyante was there. This woman's presence was like opium to me, purer, lighter, though less *substantial* than the other. But much deeper, much vaster and opening other entrances into my brain cells. This active state of spiritual exchange, this conflagration of nearby, miniscular worlds, impending, infinite lifetimes whose prospect this woman opened for me, really pointed to my life resulting in something, a reason for living in the world. For we can only accept life on condition we can be *great*, to feel at the origin of phenomena, at least at a certain number of them. Without the power to expand, without some control over things, life is unbearable. Only one thing is exciting in life: contact with the powers of the mind. However, face to face with this clairvoyante, a somewhat paradoxical phenomenon occurred. I no longer felt the need to be so powerful or vast. The fascination she exerted on me was more forceful than my pride. A certain fleeting curiosity was enough and I was ready to surrender every-

nothing bad could come from that steely blue eye with which you examined my destiny.

For me, the whole of life was transformed into that blissful landscape where the dreams which unfold arise before us with the features of our ego. The idea of absolute knowledge merged with the idea of absolute similarity between life and my conscious.

From this two-fold similarity, I got the feeling of an impending birth, where, although differing from my destiny, you were the kind, indulgent mother. Nothing appeared more mysterious to me in the fact of this abnormal second-sight, where the gestures of my past and future existence were portrayed to you, their meaning pregnant with portents and connections. I felt my mind communicated with yours as to the *form* of these portents.

But within you, Madam, what really is this parasitic fire which suddenly steals into you, through the trickery of what inconceivable environment? For you do *see*, yet the same space is displayed around us.

The horrifying part, Madam, is in the stillness of these walls, these objects, in the commonplace furniture about you, your fortunetelling props., the quiet indifference to life you share in like me.

Then your clothes, Madam, these clothes which touch a *seer*. Your flesh, in short, all your faculties. I cannot get used to the idea that you are subject to circumstances of Space, Time or that you are burdened by bodily needs. You must be much too light to exist in space.

Then again you look so lovely to me, so human, so normally graceful. As lovely as any of the women I expect

thing before her: pride, willpower, intellect. Especially intellect. The intellect I am so vain about. Naturally, I am not talking about a certain logical dexterity of the mind, quickwittedness, or the ability to make up marginal memory plans. I am talking about what is often long-term insight which does not need to materialise to fulfil itself and which is a mark of a profound attitude of mind. I have always asked people to have faith in the power of this insight, lame and more often than not immaterial though it is (which I *myself* do not possess), were they to have faith in me for a hundred years and be content with silence the rest of the time. I know what limbo this woman inhabits. I am exploring a problem which draws me close to gold, to all subtle matter, an abstract problem like pain which is formless and quivers, evaporating at the touch of a hand.

nourishment and orgasms from, who boost me up towards a physical threshold.

In my mind's eye I see you as limitless, boundless, absolutely, deeply incomprehensible. For how do you adapt to life, you who have the gift of second-sight close at hand? And that long, level road your soul roams along like a tight-rope walker where I would so clearly read the future, my death.

Yes, there are still men who know the distance between one feeling and the next, who know how to create levels and stop their desires, who know how to stand aloof from their desires and souls and return to them later as false victors. And there are those thinkers who laboriously circumscribe their ideas, who bring pretence into their dreams, those scholars who ferret out laws by means of baleful machinations!

But you, spurned, despised, soaring overhead, you set life aflame. And the wheel of Time all at once catches fire by dint of making the heavens screech.

You found me, insignificant, swept aside, rejected, as desperate as yourself and raised me up. You took me away from these surroundings, from this false universe where you do not even condescend to make the gesture of living, since you have already reached your womb of rest. And this eye, gazing on me with this unique, grieved look which is my whole existence, you magnify it and turn it in on itself. Then light blossoms forth, creating an unclouded paradise, reviving me like some mysterious wine.

HELOISE AND ABELARD

Life shrank before his eyes. Whole areas of his brain rotted. This is a known phenomenon, yet it is not simple. Abelard did not put his condition forward as a discovery but, anyway, he wrote:

My Dear Friend,

I am huge. I cannot help it, I am a summit where the

highest masts assume breasts in the shape of sails, while women feel their sexual organs turn as hard as pebbles. For my part, I cannot help feeling all these eggs haphazardly pitch and toss under their dresses according to the time and the mind. Life comes and goes, grows small through this breast-pavement. The world's aspect changes from one minute to the next. Souls with their celluloid cracks wrapped themselves around fingers and Abelard passed between the films, for the mind's erosion hung over everything.

All the teeth in all the mouths of butchered masculinity grinned at random in their dental array, whether empty or coated with hunger and plated with filth, like the frame of Abelard's mind.

But here Abelard stops. Now, only his aesophagus is working within him. Not indeed, the vertical canal's craving, its ravenous tension, but the fine, straight, silver pipe with its venular ramifications made for air, with fledgling leaves around it. In short, strictly ruffled plant life where our legs mechanically walk on and our thoughts are like tall, reefed clippers. The passage of the flesh.

The fossilised mind breaks loose. Life, fully erect, raises its head. Will the great thaw come at last? Will the bird burst through the mouths of speech, will the breasts spread out and the little mouth regain its place? Will the seed-filled tree force its way through the hand's callous granite? Yes, there is a rose in my hand and now my tongue is silent. Oh! oh! oh! how light my thought is. My mind is as slender as my hand.

But Heloise also has legs and no mistake. The best part about her is her legs. She also has that sextant-shaped thing around which all magic turns, grazes, that thing like a couched blade.

But above all Heloise has a heart. A fine, upright heart, all branches stretched, rooted, granular, braided by me, prodigal enjoyment, cataleptic in my delight.

She has hands which wrap around books with their honeyed tissue. Her breasts are so tiny; raw flesh, whose pressure drives one mad. Her breasts are a labyrinth of threads. Her thought is all mine, insinuating, twisty thought which unravels like a cocoon. She has a soul.

I am the needle flying through her thoughts and her soul takes the need and admits it. I am better in my needle than all the others in their beds, for in my bed I entwine thought and the needle in the windings of that sleeping cocoon.

For I always hark back to her, along this thread of limitless love, this universally distributed love. And craters sprout in my hands, labyrinths of breasts and explosive loves, my life overcoming sleep.

But through what trances, by what fits and starts, by what successive subsidences does he arrives at this impression of delighting in his mind. The fact is that at this moment, Abelard enjoys his own mind. He enjoys it fully. He no longer believes himself either on the one side or the other. He is there. Everything that goes on in him is his. And things are happening within him just now. Things which exempt him from seeking himself. This is the important point. He no longer has to stabilise his atoms. They unite by themselves and stratify into a single point. His whole mind is reduced to a succession of ups and downs, but always down into his heart. He has things.

His thoughts are beautiful leaves, smooth surfaces, series of nuclei, clusters of contacts and his intellect effortlessly slips between them. It goes on. That is what knowledge is: by-passing oneself. We now no longer have the problem of being delicate or being shallow or reuniting extremes or including or rejecting or separating.

He slips between these states.

He is alive. And things whirl about within him like grain between the screens.

The problem of love becomes simple.

What does it matter if he is plus or minus, since he can jump about, slide, evolve, find himself and survive.

He has rediscovered the game of love.

But how many books between his thought and the ideal!

What loss. What was his heart doing during all this time? It is surprising he has any heart left.

It is really there. It is there like a living medal, like a bush hardened into metal.

This is it. This is the nub.

Heloise is wearing a dress. She is lovely, both superficially and within.

Then he feels the elation within these roots, the massive earthly elation, one foot on the earth's rotating mass, he feels like the body of the firmament.

Abelard, having become like a dead man, feels his skeleton glaze and crack for Abelard is at the most vibrant point, at the peak of exertion and he cries out:

"Here God is sold, the vaginal plains, the fleshy pebbles are mine. No pardon, I ask no pardon. Your God is nothing but cold weight, limb dung, eye brothel, womb virgin, sky dairy."

Then the heavenly dairy exults. He is sickened.

His flesh within curdles his shell-filled silt, each hair feels stiffened, his stomach is blocked, he feels his penis liquify. Night erect and strewn with needles and then with a snip of the shears THEY eradicate his virility.

And in the distance, Heloise, quite naked, is folding her dress. Her head is white and creamy, her breasts are cloudy, her legs skinny, her teeth are chattering, making a crumpling noise, like paper. She is stupid. This is typically Abelard the eunuch's wife.

TRANSPARENT ABELARD

The sky's murmuring frame continued to trace the same amorous signs on the window pane of his soul, the same friendly messages which might perhaps save him from being a man if he consented to save himself from love.

He must give in. He cannot contain himself any longer. He gives in. This harmonious seething presses in on him. His genitals throb: a tormenting wind murmurs, making a sound higher than the heavens. The river flows with female corpses. Are they Ophelia, Beatrice or Laura? No, ink, no, wind, no, reeds, banks, shores, foam, flakes. The floodgates are down. Abelard has made floodgates out of his desire. At the juncture of the atrocious, harmonious upsurge. It is Heloise, rolling over, borne towards him—AND SHE IS VERY WILLING.

In the sky, Erasmus' hand sows bitter seeds of folly. Ah! what a strange germination. The Great Bear's motions set the time in the sky, set the sky in Time, from the reverse side of the world where the sky shows its face. Colossal relevelling.

Because the sky has a face, Abelard has a heart where so many stars sprout supreme and make his penis grow. Behind the metaphysics there is this love paved with the flesh, glowing with stones, born in the sky after so many sowings of the seeds of folly.

But Abelard swats away the heavens like blue flies. Strange rout. How can he escape? Quick, God, the eye of a needle! The smallest needle's eye through which Abelard will never be able to come looking for us.

It is a strangely fine day. It can only be fine from now on. From today, Abelard is no longer chaste. The tight book-chains are broken. He has renounced the chaste coitus permitted by God.

What a sweet thing coitus is! Although human, although enjoying a woman's body, what intimate, angelic voluptuousness! Heaven within reach of earth, less beautiful than earth. Paradise embedded in his nails.

But the appeal of sidereal lights, even from the tower's highest point, is not worth the span of a woman's thighs. Is this not priestly Abelard to whom love is so clear?

How clear coitus is, how clear the sin. So clear. What seeds, how sweet these flowers are to ecstatic sex, how insatiable the blooms of pleasure are, how pleasure spreads her poppies to the furthest extremes of enjoyment. Her poppies of sound, daylight and music, like birds swiftly, magnetically breaking cover. Pleasure plays trenchant, mystic music on the cutting edge of a slender dream: Oh!

that dream where love consents to reopen its eyes! Yes, Heloise, I walk within you, with all my philosophy, I abandon my ornaments within you and in return give you mankind whose minds shiver and glisten within you. Let mind admire itself, since Woman admires Abelard at last. Let this foam spurt against deep, dazzling walls. The Trees. Attilla's vegetation.

He has her. He possesses her. She smothers him. And each page looses its bow and advances. This book where the pages of the brain are turned.

Abelard has cut his hands. Henceforth, what symphony can equal that agonising paper kiss. Heloise swallows fire. Opens a door. Climbs the stairs. A bell rings. Her soft, flattened breasts swell up. The skin is even whiter on her breasts. Her body is white but blemished, for no woman's belly is pure. Their skins are the colour of mildew. The belly smells good but how poor. Yet so many generations dreamt of this one. Here it is. Abelard, a man, holds it. Famous belly. That's it, yet that's not it. Eat straw and fire. The kiss opens the caverns where oceans ebb and die. Here is the spasm with the heavens conspiring. A spiritual coalition breaks towards it. AND IT COMES FROM ME. Oh! how I feel as if I were nothing but guts. Without a mental overpass. Without so many magic meanings, so many superimposed secrets. She and I. We are really there. I am holding her. I kiss her. A last tension holds me back, makes me freeze. I can feel the Church complaining between my thighs, stopping me. Will it paralyse me? Am I going to withdraw? No, no. Down goes the last barrier. St. Francis of Assisi, ex-guardian of my sex, steps aside. St. Brigitta unclenches my teeth. St. Augustine undoes my belt. St. Catherine of Sienna puts God to sleep. It is over, it is really over, I am no longer a virgin. The heaven's walls are spinning round. Universal madness overcomes me. I scale my delight to the highest ethereal zeniths.

But now St. Heloise hears him. Later, infinitely later, she hears and speaks to him. A sort of night fills his teeth. Roaring, it enters the caverns of his skull. She lifts the cover on his sepulchre with her insect-spindly hand. As if you were listening to a goat in a dream. She is trembling, but he is trembling far more than her. Poor man! Poor Antonin Artaud! This impotent wretch is really him, who, having scaled the stars, tried to pit his weakness against the cardinal points of the elements. Who, with each of the subtle or static appearances of nature, endeavours to compose one thought which holds together, one idea which holds water. If he could, he would create as many elements or at least provide the metaphysics of disaster, starting with the fall.

Heloise is sorry that in the place of her belly she did not have a wall like the one she was leaning against when Abelard pricked her with his obscene sting. For Artaud, privation is the beginning of the death he desires. But what a fine picture: a eunuch!

UCCELLO THE HAIR

For Génica

Uccello, my friend, my fantasy, you lived with this myth about hair. The shadow of that great lunar hand whereby you imprint the fantasies of your brain will never reach your ear's vegetation, which turns and teems leftward with all the drifts of your heart. The hairs are left, Uccello, dreams are sinister, as are nails and the heart. The shades all open sinister as human orifices, naves. With your head resting on that table where the whole of humanity capsizes, how could you see anything else but the huge shadow of a hair. A hair like two forests, like three finger-nails, a meadow of eyelashes, like a rake in the sky's grasses. Choked and hanged people, eternally staggering about on the plains of that flat table-top on which your heavy head is bowed. And near you, when you examine facets, what do you see but the branching circulation, a latticework of veins, the tiniest trace of a wrinkle, the floral tracework of a sea of hair. Everything turning, everything vibratile and what is the eye worth stripped of its lashes. Wash, wash those eyelashes, Uccello, wash away the lines, wash away the quivering trace of hairs and wrinkles on the hanging, egg-like faces of the dead watching you, and in your monstrous palm, full of moonlight, as if lit by spleen, here again the majestic trace of your hair becomes visible with its lines as fine as dreams in your drowned man's brain. How many secrets and how many surfaces from one hair to the next? But two hairs, one next to the other, Uccello. The repeated, duplicated, inexpressibly fine, ideal hair line. There are some wrinkles which go around the face and extend down as far as the neck, but there are lines under the hair as well, Uccello. You can also travel right around this egg suspended between the stones and stars, alone possessing the dual animation of sight.

When you painted your two friends and yourself on a well-applied canvas, you left something like the suggestion of a strange woolliness on the canvas and in this, Paolo Uccello, though badly lit, I was able to detect your regrets and sorrows. Wrinkles, Paolo Uccello, are snares, but the hair is a living language. In one of your paintings, Paolo Uccello, I saw the glimmer of a tongue in the luminescent shadow of the teeth. A tongue helps you recapture a living expression in a lifeless canvas. And because of that, Uccello, all interspersed through your beard, I saw you had understood and portrayed me beforehand. May you be blessed, you who had a rugged, grass-roots preoccupation with perspective. You lived with this idea as if in a vivid poison. And you are eternally going round within the circles of this idea and I hound you down, groping along, using as a thread the light of this tongue calling me from the bottom of a miraculously healed mouth. Preoccupied with perspective in a rugged, grass-roots way, I who lack roots at every stage. Did you really assume I would descend into this underworld with my mouth open and my mind everlastingly astonished. Did you assume these screams would penetrate all people's and language's senses, like those of a madly reeled off thread? The great patience of old age is what saved you from a premature death. For I do know you were born with a mind as empty as mine, but you were able to set this mind on something even less than the trace and birth of a filament. You are balancing by a hair's breadth over a dread abyss, and yet you are separated from it for ever.

But also, Uccello, little boy, little bird, little tattered luminary, I bless that well-placed silence of yours. Apart from those lines your mind commands, like a bower of messages, there is nothing left of you, only silence and the secret of your fastened robe. Two or three signs in the air. What man could claim to be more alive than these three signs and, hour after hour that envelope him, could we dream of craving more than the silence which precedes or follows them. I feel all the world's stones and the illuminations in space my journey produced, make their way through me. They form the words of a black syllable within the pastures of my brain. You, Uccello, you are learning to be just a line and the elevated degree of a secret.

THE ANVIL OF STRENGTH

These discharges, nausea, lashes. *These* are the things where Fire starts. Tongues and their fire. Fire woven into coiled tongues in the shimmering of the earth, opening up like a belly in labour, with its honey and sugar bowels. All this soft belly's obscene wound yawns open, but the fire gapes above it with burning, tortuous tongues, with vents as if thirsting at the tips. This fire entwined like clouds in limpid water and beside it the light delineates a rule and filaments. And the earth half open, everywhere, revealing arid secrets. Secrets like surfaces. The earth and its guts and its prehistoric solitude, the earth's primitive formations where the world's strata are uncovered in coal-black shadows.—The earth gives birth beneath the icy fires. See the fire in the Three Rays, with the crowning of its mane where eyes teem. Eyes, millions of millipedes of them. The convulsed, incandescent centre of this fire is like a thunderclap's quartered lance at the firmament's summit. The white-hot convulsive centre. Pure explosiveness in a clash of strength. Force's terrible lance which shatters in totally blue reverberations.

The Three Rays fan out, their spokes plummet down and converge on the same centre. This centre is a whiteish disc covered with a spiral of eclipses.

The shadows of this eclipse form a barrier on the zigzags of the heaven's towering masonry.

But above the sky is the Double-Horse. When conjured up, the horse is steeped in the light of strength, on the background of a ragged wall and constricted to its very ligaments. The ligament between its twin breasts. And within it, the first of these two is much stranger than the other. Brilliance is concentrated in it, while the second is only a plodding shadow of that brilliance.

Lower yet than the wall's shadow, the horse's head and breast form a shadow as if all the waters of the world ran up the mouth of a well.

The open fan dominates a pyramid of peaks, a vast harmony of summits. A hint of the desert hangs over these summits and above them a dishevelled star floats, hovering, inexplicably, horribly. Suspended like the good in man, or the evil in man's relations to man, or death in life. Stellar rotatory force.

But behind this ultimate vision, this network of plants, stars, ground slashed to the bone, behind this fiery, germinal flocculation, this questioning geometry, this rotating network of summits. Behind this socket fixed in the mind and this mind whose tissue emerges, uncovering its deposits, thus behind this man's hand who imprints his hard thumb and outlines its trials and errors, behind this mixture of manipulation and brains and these wells in all the senses of the soul and these caverns in reality, rises the Town with its fortified walls, the enormously high Town where all the heavens are not too great to serve as its roof, where plants grow upside down with the speed of projected stars.

This town of caves and walls which throws out filled archways and cellars like bridges over the bottomless chasm.

How we would like to put an enormously large shoulder into the vault of these arches and to the arcature of these bridges, a shoulder with blood spreading from it. And rest one's body and one's head teeming with dreams on the edge of these giant cornices where the sky rises in tiers.

For up above is a Biblical sky where white clouds fly. But what soft threats in these clouds. What storms. Allowing the flakes of fire from this Sinai to pierce through. Then what about the earth's cast shadow and the muffled, chalky lighting. And after all, what about that shadow in the form of a goat and that ram! And that Sabbath of Constellations.

A cry to summon all that and a tongue to hang myself from it.

All this ebb and flow starts in me.

Show me the earth's insertion, my mind's hinges, the awful genesis of my nails. A mass, a huge mass of falsehood separates me from my delusions. And this mass is any colour you like.

The world flows over it like the rocky sea, and I with the ebb of love.

Dogs, have you done rolling your pebbles over my soul. Me. Me. Turn the page of rubble. I also await heaven's gravel and boundless beaches. This fire must start with me. This fire, these tongues, and the caverns of my conception. Let the icebergs return and beach under my teeth. I have a hard head, but I have a smooth soul and a heart made of wrecked matter. I lack meteors, and bellows ablaze, my throat seeks to speak names and something like the vibrating filament of objects. The smell of nothingness, an absurd stench, the dung of all death. . . . Light, subtle humour. I am also only waiting for the wind. Whether called love or misery, it can hardly fail to run me aground on a beach of bones.

THE PERSONAL AUTOMATON

to Jean de Bosschère

He said he saw a great preoccupation with sex in me. But taut sexual organs, swollen like an object. An object made of metal and boiling lava, filled with rootlets, with boughs caught by the air.

The astounding genital calmness filled with so much scrap iron. Air gathers around the iron from every direction.

And above them a fiery growth, a meagre, tangled pasture which takes root in this bitter mould. And it grows with ant-like gravity, an ant-hill foliage forever digging deeper into the earth. This heinously black foliage grows and digs down, and as it delves, it seems as if the earth grows distant, that the ideal centre of everything gathers about a progressively more slender point.

But all this quivering in a body laid out with the play of all its organs, its legs, its arms with their automatic relays and round about them the buttocks' curves encircling the secured genitals. A flight of arrows shot from outside the canvas are aimed at these organs whose sexuality increases, in which sexuality is endlessly gathering head. Just as in the branches of my mind there is this physical, sexual barrier which is there like a torn-out page, like a strip torn from the flesh, like an aperture of thunder and lightning on the smooth casing of the heavens.

But elsewhere there is this woman seen from behind, sufficiently resembling the silhouette of the traditional witch.

But her *weight* is foreign to tradition and rules. She unfurls like a sort of wild bird in the shadows she gathers about her, using them as a sort of thick cloak.

The very rippling of the cloak is such a powerful sign that just its fluttering is enough to denote the witch and the night in which she unfurls. This night is in relief and in depth and, in the very line which travels from the eye, a marvellous deck of cards scatters as if suspended on a pool. Light from the depths catches the corners of the cards. And unnaturally abundant clovers float like black insects' wings.

The depths haven't settled enough yet to stop any idea of a fall. They are like the first landing of an ideal fall, the bottom being hidden by the painting itself.

There is a type of giddiness whose spinning has difficulty in emerging from the dark, a ravenous descent swallowed up in some sort of night.

And as if to give full meaning to this giddiness, to this whirling hunger, a mouth opens wide, gapes, seems to want to connect with the four corners of the horizon. A mouth like the stamps of life to cancel out darkness and the fall, to give a radiant outlet to the vertigo which drains everything towards the depths.

The coming of swarming night with its train of sewers. That is the place where this painting is located: at the sewer discharge pipe.

A murmuring wind stirs all these lost larvae as night gathers them in shimmering images. We sense the pounding of floodgates, a sort of awful volcanic shock where daylight dissociated itself. And from this shock, from two principles ripping apart thus, all powerful imagery is born on a tide livelier than a ground swell.

Are there so many things in this painting?

This is the power of a set dream, as hard as an insect's shell and full of feet darted through all the points in the sky.

And in relief, on these convulsed shoals, on this energising light blending in with all the metals of night, the very picture of the eroticism of the shades, arises the obscene titanic silhouette of the Personal Automaton.

A great pile and a great fart.

It hangs from wires but only its joints are ready and the air's throbbing actuates the rest of its body. Night gathers round it like a meadow, like a grove of black boughs.

The contrast is secret here, it is like a scalpel line. It is suspended by a razor's edge, in the inverted realm of souls.

Let us turn the page.

The head is a stage higher. And a green explosion of fire-damp, like a huge match, slashes and rends the air at this spot where the head is not.

I find myself exactly the same as when I see myself in the world's mirrors, resembling a house or a table since resemblance is something else.

If we could go behind the façade what disjointure we would see, what a veinous massacre. Gutted corpses, piled up.

The whole thing as high as a plate of shrimps.

This is the lineament so much mental activity resulted in.

Besides, this rings hollow, in the end, for how I look on sex, for which my appetite has not yet died.

After so many checks and abatements, after all these flayed corpses, after the warning of the black clovers, after the witches' banners, after that cry from a mouth in the bottomless chasm, after having run into barriers, after this swirl of stars, this tangle of roots and hair, I am not disgusted enough for all these experiences to deprive me of it.

Experience's precipitous walls do not divert me from my main delectation.

At the basis of revolutionary outbursts and storms, at the basis of this pounding in my brain, in this abyss of desires and questions, despite so many problems,—so many fears, in the most treasured part of my head I retain this preoccupation with sex which petrifies me and rips out my blood.

I may have blood of iron slippery blood full of swamps, I may be stung by plagues and repudiations, infected and assailed by degradation and horror, provided the soft shield of my iron-hard penis continues. I made it with iron, filled it with honey, and they were always the same organs in the midst of these bitter foothills. These are the organs where the rapids meet, where thirsts sink deep.

Filled with anger, without calm or forgiveness, my torrents grow ever greater and deeper and furthermore, in addition, I add threats and the hardness of stars and firmaments.

This painting, like a world in the flesh, a raw world full of fibres and thongs, where the irritating force of fire lacerates the inner heavens, ripping the intellect open, where primitive powers expand, where states we cannot name appear in their purest manifestation, the least suspected of real alloys.

It is the sulphurated life of consciousness coming up into daylight with its dim lights and stars, its lairs, its firmament,

with the vivaciousness of pure desire,

with its call to constant death bordering on the membrane of resurrection.

Woman's body is there, on obscene display, with its wooden frame. Closed, unchanging wood. The wood of excited desire, its very irritation chilled by its dry clinical nakedness. First the buttocks and to the rear all the great, massive rump, there like an animal's hindquarters where the head has only the importance of a pin. The head is there as the idea of a head, as the expression of a trifling, forgotten part.

To the right and lower down, in the distant background, held in reserve, like the topmost point of the sign of the cross.

Shall I describe the rest of the painting?

It seems to me this body places itself just by appearing. On this dry ground, just on the surface, there is all the depth of an ideal perspective existing only in the mind. We discover, like a feature, zig-zag lightning scars right in the earth and cards dance around there.

Above and below, the Pythoness, the sorceress, like a sort of angel, a kindly dragon, with her decrescent face. All the mind's snails gnaw at her abstract face and turn about like a plaited ligament.

Above and below. Above, her face is that of a hollow mummy. Below is her bulk with her huge, clearly outlined figure. She is there like the walls of night, solid, bewitching, displaying the fire of the sulphurated cards.

A host of hearts, a host of clovers, like so many signs, so many calls.

Have I a coat, have I a robe?

Night dungeon-like, ink-filled darkness, unrolls its badly cemented walls.

THE WINDOW OF LOVE

I wanted her shimmering with flowers, with little volcanoes attached to her armpits and especially that bitter cystic lava at the core of her body, standing erect.

There was also an eyebrow arch and the entire sky passed under it. A sky truly full of rape, kidnapping, lava; a storm and fury sky, in short, an utterly theological sky. A sky like a standing arch, like the trumpet of doom, like hemlock drunk in dreams, a sky contained in all the phials of death, a Heloise above Abelard sky, a loving suicide sky, a sky possessing all the furies of love.

This sky was a protestor's sin, sin held back at confession, those sins which burden the conscience of priests, a truly theological sin.

And I loved her.

She was a maid, in a Hoffmanesque tavern, but a shabby, sluttish little girl, an unwashed slut of a serving girl. She dished out the plates, cleaned up, made the beds, swept the rooms, shook the canopies over the beds, and undressed in front of her attic window like all the maids in all Hoffmann's tales.

At the time, I slept in a sorry bed whose mattress rose up every night, curled up in the face of the advancing rats thrown up by the ebbing of bad dreams, and smoothed out again at sun rise. My sheets smelt of tobacco and the morgue, and that deliciously nauseating smell investing our bodies when we concentrate on smelling them. In short, real amorous student's sheets.

I was swotting away at a voluminous, blundering thesis on The Miscarriages of the Human Mind at the Soul's worn-out Thresholds Man's Mind never attains.

But I was much more obsessed by thoughts of the girl than all the visions of the excessive nominalism of objects.

I saw her through the sky, through the broken windows in my room, through her own eyebrows, through the eyes of all my old flames and through my mother's golden hair.

Now it was New Year's Eve. The thunder was thundering, the lightning was flashing, the rain was coming along fine, the cocoons of dreams were bleating, the frogs in all the ponds were croaking, in short, the night was doing its job.

I now had to find a way of getting in touch with reality. . . . It was not enough to be in touch with the dark vibrations of objects, for example, to hear the voices of the volcanoes, to invest the object of my love with all the charms of preconceived adultery for example, or in all the horror, filth, scatology, crime and deceit connected with the idea of love. I simply had to find a means of approaching her openly, that is to say and above all, *to speak to her.*

The window suddenly opened. In one corner of the room I saw huge chess pieces with an array of hidden lights reflected on them. Bodiless heads danced in circles, knocked together, fell about like nine pins. There was an enormous wooden Knight, a morphine Queen, a Castle of love and an age to come. Hoffmann's hands moved the pawns and each pawn said: DO NOT SEEK HER THERE. And there were angels in the sky whose wings refused to budge. I therefore stopped looking out of my window, or hoping to see my beloved little maid.

In the room just above mine I heard feet finish crushing planetary crystals. Passionate sighs came through the floor and I heard something soft slump down.

At that instant all the plates on earth came clattering down and all the customers in the world's restaurants gave chase to the little Hoffmannesque serving girl. Then the maid appeared, running like the devil, then Pierre Mac Orlan, the absurd boot-repairer passed by, pushing a barrow down the road. After him came Hoffmann holding an umbrella, then Achim d'Arnim, then Lewis walking obliquely. At length, the earth opened and Gérard de Nerval appeared.

He was greater than all the rest. There was also a little man, me.

"You are not dreaming, mind you," said Gérard de Nerval, "besides, here is Monk Lewis who knows something about it. Lewis, would you venture to maintain the opposite?"

"No, by all the hairy twats."

I thought—they are stupid, what is the use of regarding them as great authors.

"So you see," said Gérard de Nerval, "this is all related. You mix her up, season her to taste, don't think twice, peel her off, the girl is my wife."

I thought—he does not even know the importance of words.

"Excuse me. The value. The value of words," my brain whispered to me as it knew something about it, too.

"Shut up, brain," I said, "you are not bright enough yet."

Hoffmann said to me:

LET US GET TO THE POINT.

And I said:

"I don't know how to get together with her, I don't dare to."

"Well, you don't have to be daring," Lewis retorted, "you will win her OBLIQUELY."

"Obliquely, only to what?" I replied, "for the time being she is the one who keeps crossing my mind."

"But we've told you love is devious, life is devious, thought is devious, everything is devious. YOU WILL HAVE HER WHEN YOUR MIND IS NOT ON HER."

Listen. Up there. Can't you hear that soft conspiracy, the contact of that inconceivably plastic mass?

My head was splitting.

At last I understood they were her breasts. I understood they were touching. My little maid, her very bosom, had breathed all those sighs. I also understood she had lain down on the floor to be nearer me.

The rain continued to flow.
Down in the street they sang ghastly, stupid songs:

At my love's it's sweet
Gobbling up chick-weed (bis)
Some are roosters
Some are chicks
At my love's it's sweet
Dovey on her love-seat
All the moisture of her tits
Is not worth the pips
Of her amorous heat.

"Stupid swine," I yelled, getting up, "you are spoiling the true spirit of love."

The street was empty. There was only the moon which kept up its watery murmur.

Which charms are finest, which jewels costliest, which almonds the most succulent?

I smiled at the thought.

"I am not the devil, as you see!" she said.

Well, no, she wasn't the devil. My little maid was in my arms.

"I wanted you for such a long time, such a long time," she said.

Then we took leave of darkest night. The moon climbed back up in the sky, Hoffmann burrowed down into his cellar, all the restaurateurs put up the covers, there was nothing left, only love. Heloise and her coat, Abelard and his tiara, Cleopatra and her aspic, all the tongues of darkness, all the stars of madness.

Then love was like an ocean, like sin, like life, like death.

Love under the arcades, pelvic love, love in bed, love like clinging ivy, love like a tidal wave.

Love as great as told in tales, love like art, love like everything which exists.

And all this in so small a woman, in such a mummified heart, in such a limited mind, but mine *thought* for both of us.

From the depths of some unfathomable intoxication, a painter seized with dizziness suddenly despaired. But the night was lovelier than anything else. All the students returned to their rooms, the artist painted over his cypresses. My thoughts were more and more suffused with Domesday light.

Soon there was only a gigantic mountain of ice left and on it blonde hair dangling down.

PART TWO

UNPUBLISHED PROSE AND POETRY

THE ASSUMPTION

The steps were snatched up, as if carried away by the team's giddy speed and Monseigneur's seventeen horses broke into a mad gallop. A salvo was fired from the Palace; the horn blew, wailing.

At that very moment Monsieur stepped out of his room, dressed all in black with a look of doom. His three children cried. At almost the same instant, the Chapel door opened up allowing the prior, accompanied by two lacqueys in hyacinth livery, to pass stormily through. Carrying a little black casket of glistening lacquer, they swiftly moved down the topmost steps, then the Master clapped his hands.

There was then an incredible silence. Spectrally motionless, the mysterious, dumb puppets froze and soft unreal light replaced the languid turquoise of the skies. Suddenly the noise of the coach nearby rattled the window panes.

Monsieur clenched his two shrunken hands to the dry skin of his face, the prior and his two servants vanished and the embers of the dying day, in dumb terror, filtered through the thick panes of the trembling lattice windows. At last, in the flashing gleams of a forest of torches and the frightening din of the iron-bound wheels, Monseigneur entered among us.

Then the silence became so painfully solemn our throats constricted and all the women cried.

Terrors welled our pores and at first no words were spoken.

Monsieur bowed, stepped forward, then stopped. No one dared look. Then Monseigneur looked around the room at length and a great Bible was brought.

Some hours later, an array of lacqueys thronged the approach to the coach. They looked at one another, stumbling like drunken men along the steps outside where high lanterns burned, carrying chests, mattocks, arms and clothing. The glass doors were unhinged and taken away. Unusual activity disturbed the oppressive night and the servants hurried.

But the moment the new day dispelled the darkness, there was a bustle of activity around Madame's rooms. Maidservants went by carrying linen and soon Madame herself, all in white and as pale as death, fell prey to a strange, agonizing attack, seized by compulsive trembling. The great flames from the torches lit up like veils in the air. She appeared to come to life again and sighed. But she looked more like her own corpse than Madame.

At this point the prior appeared, his cassock strangely dirty, with a look of unutterable dismay, and the two acolytes with priestly robes, stepping like sleepwalkers. Two or three doors banged round about the silence from on high and suddenly the voices of the children rose with shrill resonance, funereally intoning.

A dark pursuit made the stone work quiver and the noise of a struggle arose. Suddenly Monseigneur, all bloody, appeared below the steps. He tottered. Then swords were brandished on all sides and the torches that had fallen over flared up on the floor boards. The carnage swelled into dizziness around Monsieur, as he fought, wounded.

But Monseigneur had smiled. Something like unhoped-for dew dispersed the universal fury. Like a curtain rising. Monseigneur, who had assumed ineffable child's eyes, looked at us. The sun's wheel threw out all its flames. The solemn morning unfolded. Inexpressible contentedness seeped through our floral hands and wind filled our robes like sails, like the water in distended stones. But the turning of this ineffable wheel constantly brought our thoughts back in the same ecstatic circle, where our recollections dissolved. The sky fell back like a mirror and the whole of the great castle spread out in its crystals. There was only a sort of gentle shepherd left, gazing on three dead sheep.

THE USHER WITH BLUE GLASSES

When he took us out in the woods carpeted by autumn, he tried to make us pursue the setting sun—he hung back an instant among the dead leaves. But the day had already declined, turning that tree in the background orange. The steeple rotated in a yellow ray with the softness of a sigh—then the earth steamed and we turned back.

His face had once again become impassive, as if turned inward, and set. Once again he had become distant and often until the bed-time bell went, he never touched a book or said a word and his two hands seem clasped on the edge of the desk as they shone in the light from the lamp.

Something pure and detached came over his whole being and we would have liked to think well of him. But we would have to have seen his eyes. He worried us. That clerical habit of joining his hands, his walk, his squat, heavy stance as if bent double, gave him an extraordinary appearance among men.

And then, how he would suddenly call out our names and scoff at us, enjoying our credulity, then relapse into that absent-minded, distant manner towards us!

Then when the books piled up on his table and he worked away with his pen, if we were unlucky enough to stir, he turned on us with such a ferocious look that something heavier than fear weighed down on us.

The college arose like a citadel on the edge of the old town, in a part where the earth swelled up, so much so that on one side, the plane trees formed an enormous green crown around it and their leaves swayed right under the windows of our study. Doubtless we followed the changing seasons in the tree tops with interest, dramatic falls of rain, and the skies, the sun or lightning as framed by the windows, but this opening onto the outside world seemed to exercise the fascination of a real spell over the usher. Sometimes he stared out for hours, and on days when there was a strong wind his head swayed in time with the heightened rhythms of the trees and he seemed to mumble lulling words.

But starting from the day when the striking adolescent whose presence so impressed itself on our youth sat among us, a look of sadness, daily more disconsolate, modelled his stony features and sometimes his face, as if questioning, turned to where the child sat.

From that day on, his little room re-echoed with the sound of a languid violin, reminding us of stories, though we had forgotten what they were about. Now and then, as we passed his door, other sounds also wafted out, old lullabies—sung in a hoarse, quavering voice, evil as well, yes, one might have said, implacable. Then again after the hours of service, the organ sometimes intoned.

One morning the child did not come. The usher took the study period as usual and the afternoon class was about to end when the rumour spread through the school that woodcutters had found the body of a pallid child in the woods which (sheltered) our outings. It did not take long to identify this as our wonderful schoolfellow.

Then with our minds in an uproar, we were momentarily numb with fear. But we were already on our feet, everyone in the disrupted class stood up as terrifying cries uttered by an inhuman voice filled the school. And at that moment the organ intoned.

There was a mad escape down the halls and the stairs were hammered, trampled by the feet of three hundred panic-stricken children.

The noise brought us right to the usher's door, just in time to hear these words exclaimed in the same superhuman voice: "The child, take the child away!"—then silence.

The door was broken open, but our poor usher already lay stretched out on the ground, his eyes in death, with a broken phial of laudanum beside him on the floor.

PSYCHIC EXCURSION

Magic starts with incantation. The word magic, as understood by most, vaguely gives rise to the idea of occult practices able to waken the dark powers of nature and to subjugate the very phantoms of death. This is partly true.

The haziness of phantasms in man's intellect which prompts the idea of recapturing, with the help of words at least, of conjuring up these marvellous powers seemingly reserved for the few, is not just wish-fulfillment. In any case it has given us those jewels of world literature, *The Thousand and One Nights*, *Perrault's Tales*, *The Tales of Hoffmann* and among others, *The Golden Bowl* and *Poe's Tales*. Nor is it just the act of uncovering the relationships between the things invented, to juggle with time, distance and opposing elements.

Rather it is the whole of the quasi-historic practices, the explicit attributes of such fabulous characters, this gallery of human phantoms called magicians, sorcerers, dervishes, fakirs, their incongruous garb, the mysterious vegetation and the beginning of all this, the Sabbath.

Yet if the greater majority of men wanted to give themselves the trouble to draw up a detailed account of their remarks about this, how many would be able to sift their truly general, truly human ideas out of all this confused mass, or clearly to formulate what they imagine all this phantasmagoria to be. For the greater part of them, all humanity's magic heroes are contained in *The Secrets of The Great Albert*, that treat for hysterical cooks, and for the others who give themselves the trouble to think about it and who say to themselves: if there were any magicians, what would they get up to? They confuse them with real chemical scientists or even with ordinary conjurors. We do not know if any magicians ever existed in the course of ages, such as sprout up everywhere from the hallowed soil of *The Thousand and One Nights*.

Today, aside from a few children, no one believes in magicians any more. None the less, one thing is remarkable: all these miraculous tales only rarely deal with phantasms of the dead, or so slightly as to be of no value.

None the less, we might hit upon the secret of divine ascendancy and the mental configuration of the world through investigating death, whatever Maeterlinck may say about it in his sad, cruel, *Great Secret.* Indeed it is not very likely that intellects, purified by the great shedding of their bodily shells, entering the great totality of the mind, returning to this great original, subtle totality, should be able to pierce the arcana of the origin of things and their fate.

We already possess this means of ranging through death here and now with the occurrence of hypnosis, which frees the subconscious and its vitreous features within us and sends it to frolic free on the edges of the other world. We cannot be sure that death, in rendering our souls more sensitive to the mental apperception of the beyond, begins by a lurid aping of sleep, or that, through progressively dulling the mind, separates it from the body. I imagine in death there must be the anxiety sleeping men suffer, who ask themselves agonizingly if they are really dreaming. A maddening question!

It is fairly clear that it would make little difference to man if he could reverse the elemental order, if he had no hold over the giddy unleashing of the phantasms of death. The Egyptians knew the words and the powers to hold the soul back on the borders of Life. Magic's unbelievable fascination over man comes from this miraculous power. Incantation was eventually used to intercept the brute forces of nature, but Magic's great effectiveness lies in the subjugation of Death.

THE POOR MUSICIAN'S ASTONISHING ADVENTURE

Hoichi, an excellent musician, who, as ill-luck would have it, was blind, also had fine ears, as red as the setting sun, which he lost one night in old Japan, as follows.

The business first began one evening shortly after sundown, in front of the dazzling gate of the Danamosura Temple, where Hoichi, the poor musician, had charitably been given shelter. Hoichi could not see the twinkling sky, nor the waters beside which the old temple stood, but the moving magic of the night's advance imparted a sighing to the air and something like the sound of invisible presences. The blind man sensed the flight of hidden demons, the legendary *hike* who made him mysteriously shiver as they passed by. He was afraid. The empty temple slept. At times the water breathed a sigh similar to those of the deceased. Huddled up, clutching his biva tightly, his face averted, pressed against the thin wall, he waited. At that instant, the commanding voice of the Samurai called him, as if breathed by the essence of things. It called a first time, then a second. And as Hoichi still gave no answer, the invisible Samurai drew near. Hoichi felt a metal hand grip his. The warrior seemed to be very strong and heavily armed. He therefore obeyed.

"I have come," said the warrior, "I have come. . . ."

And they walked on amidst the silent rocks.

Then the great, distant, commanding voice continued with the same sound of clanging music:

"From my master, from my master, to fetch you."

And as the rocks relapsed into silence, the leaves whispered.

The way was unaccountably long, but what frightened the blind musician most was the purpose of this unexplained journey, from which he felt he would never have the courage to escape. At last they arrived before a high gate in front of which his guide stopped him.

"My master," he told him, "expects a song on your biva, from you, O most wonderful of earthly musicians, lovelier than any you would sing to the greatest Emperor on earth. My master, greater than the greatest Emperor." He lapsed into silence. Then the gates opened and they heard hurrying steps like those of a great trampling crowd and they arrived at what seemed to the musician to be a staircase. It appeared screens were being drawn aside, whispers arose like flights of wild geese in sudden gusts of breath. An impression of dazzling lights touched the blind singer's skin. He felt he was in a brightly lit palace. But the staggering terror which prickled his skin made his head reel at each step.

"Sing for us, sing for us," began the voice of the Samurai cased in armour; "sing about the Princess's marriage, our great Emperor's Princess." Then it seemed to the poor bard as if his sight had returned. It was as if his eyelids had lifted, as if his limbs had been transformed into glass. He had the impression of falling and he felt his fingers run across the strings of his biva, now alive, in accordance with the rhythms of the poem they bade him sing and pictures formed around him, lovely, wonderful like dreams born on the ocean bed. He saw sumptuous processions dissolve, astonishing flowers fade away and the legendary faces of maidens vanish in the fires of miraculous hearths. He even felt his head turning. Then he fell back, he wanted to die, he felt such intense emotions they were more than he could bear. But with the speed of lightning the Samurai had got up, crossed the space between the palace and the gates, and had reached the road—and was following him. Shortly before dawn, they were back in front of the little temple beside the water. Hoichi turned around three times and listened. Once again he was blind and alone. Then he dared to question himself for the first time that night and he asked himself: WHERE HAVE I BEEN?

Now the priest who had sheltered him returned about dawn to take up his duties and was greatly surprised that morning to find the musician flat against the temple wall in the same position and in the same place as when he had left the evening before.

He neither spoke nor moved until twilight first began, and when they tugged at his sleeve or shook him to get him to eat or tried to get him to stand up, he fell to the ground limp as a rag doll, so much so the priest thought him dead. Then he called for bearers and mourners and sent messengers to the town and began to keep vigil. The shadows of the trees grew terrifyingly. Night covered the earth. Then called by some supernatural spirit or other, the blind musician got up. . . . He appeared so unconscious of his movements he seemed to be sleep-walking, as if guided by an unknown hand. The little priest was soon out of breath following him. Besides, he was very frightened. At times, he wiped his mouth or one eye and pulled his little robe up as it slipped out of his fingers at every step. In this fashion they arrived before the old gates of the town cemetery. Then the little priest fell back. He dropped to his knees in terror. He felt he had reached the utmost limits of life. The gates had opened. He seemed to hear the clash of armies. He heard the trumpeting of imaginary elephants, and the musician lay on the flag stones within a tomb, his face ecstatic, and seeming to witness a display of mysterious fairylands, he struck his biva in sudden fits.

Shortly before dawn they were back on the path to the remote temple. The exhausted musician, as if sobered, shuffled along, led by the priest. "You are bewitched, Hoichi," he said, "you are bewitched. You have come under the spell of evil spirits, Hoichi, you have . . . you have GONE BEYOND LIFE. Take care you don't disappear into the beyond completely. They are torturing you, my friend, you would vanish in torment." So they went on, the shuffling musician and the priest, the little priest taking little steps, leading him along.

"Do not be afraid, tonight I will clothe you in the cloak-of-protection, the magic clothing which turns evil spirits away."

This they did and, as the evening drew on, the priest helped by an acolyte, undertook the office of undressing the musician and on his skin they drew the exorcisms which drive away evil spirits. Covered with inscriptions in this way, he looked as if he were clothed in black lace. They covered his face, his limbs, his whole body, then, as it was getting late, they left. And the musician, once more overcome with terror as he regained consciousness, huddled up, waiting. Dark birds skimmed overhead. Distant junks creaked on the water. He felt his head sink down between his shoulders at each noise breathed by the night. He wished he were deaf. He wished he would lose consciousness. He would have liked to be dead.—Suddenly the Samurai's great metallic voice sounded. Then he hunched up, he was shaken by a prolonged tremor and he felt the hair on his scalp tingling. But the Samurai seemed to hesitate. He circled about as if at a loss. Then Hoichi heard him stamp with rage. "Hoichi," he cried, "Hoichi, they are waiting for you at the palace, waiting for you to go on with your story. Hoichi, where are you, Hoichi?" He suddenly stopped. "By the gods," he cried, "if I can't see the musician, at least I can see his ears. I will take them back to my master to prove I have carried out my mission." He therefore drew near the place where the musician lay prostrate and where he could see only his two ears—and he ripped them off.

The priest had neglected to paint any guardian verses on his ears.

And that was how Hoichi, the poor musician, lost his ears.

OUTLINE OF A NEW EDUCATIONAL PROGRAMME

MATRICULATION
REASONING FROM EXAMPLES

PART I

I. The Laws of History: the accession of dynasties, revolutions, political assassinations—famous examples, causes and discussions.

II. Comparative Civilisations: customs and morals here and abroad, housing and dress.

III. Circumstances of the Great Discoveries: the Americas, the Poles, the Monsoon which drove the Hovas to Madagascar.

IV. Psychology of the Great Conquerors: their habits, passions, character—the great scientists, the great poets, the great reformers.

V. The great human myths—the solar myth, the Holy Trinity, Isis and Osiris.
Comparative Mythology: Greek, Roman, Indian,

Japanese, Lapp, Egyptian, Aztec, Eskimo. . . . Comparative religion.

VI. Source literature; texts to be explained.

VII. The psychology of the emotions as born out by major human facts:
motives for killing, lying, stealing, suicide, drunkenness, love, poisoning.

VIII. The great laws of nature; winds, storms, cataclysms. . . .

IX. First Principles of Comparative Philosophy.

X. Elementary Arithmetic and Algebra.

PART II

I. Elementary Natural History, Evolution, Transformism, Biology.

II. Elementary Geology and Cosmography.

III. Psychology, Ethics, Aesthetics, Metaphysics.

IV. The Principal Philosophic Systems.

V. First Principle of Physics and Chemistry.

VI. Elementary Anatomy and Physiology.

VII. Basic Medicine and Psychiatry.

VIII. Commerce, Industry, Protectionism, Free Trade, some figures.

BRIEF SKETCH OF PAINTING SINCE 1850

We call him brutish Courbet because when treating painted subjects, he illustrated the whys and wherefores of what I might call the development of his sentient self less than others. Cézanne was more intelligent and we will refer to him later. Courbet's realism was not pure. He was motivated by too many rather unconscious impulses commonly called instinct as slaves to nature. All talented realists are romantics at heart, an appearance of frenzy which colours the brush.

Some regard Courbet as a painter of animals. His urban

landscapes are unrivalled in boredom. He painted a very few flat scenes of life which the critics praised. *The Funeral at Ornans, the Studio, the Fireman* from some place or other. All in all, a bodger who by applying himself, succeeded in squeezing some blood and soul out of the muck of dismal stuff.

What else did Manet do except to combine a more modern approach, more subtle tonal tremors and a very present-day sense of line with full-scale plagiarism from Velasquez. Also something a little tainted, a little mouldy, to an art which having reached its apogee, stopped. Impressionism was able to modify its technique late in life, but it never added anything to its temper. Besides, real impressionism lies elsewhere.

ART AND GREATNESS

Art is always a high point to be attained, Monticelli called it the High C of colour. In fact, it is fairly clear that beauty never exists without a certain greatness, a certain solemnity. We speak grandly of small things and grandiosely of great things. Beauty comes from something, outside the work, as it were, yet which is contained in it, an invisible presence. It is also simple. It never knows short-lived success, an hour's brief pleasure which gives an air of beauty to something that did not aim at it. It is the long-lost brother, the prodigal returned to his father, the friend who had dropped out of sight. It is something which has an unerring place in the present, the frame hung on our day-to-day walls. I am not referring to beauty, period, but to the majesty of undisputed works (Giotto, Cimabue, Cranach, Breughel, Téniers, Watteau and Le Nain). Who cannot see that the beauty of these works does not stem from the ease of their execution or the felicities in their colouring, or the just balance of their different grounds . . . does not stem from . . . does not stem from. . . . For as I am speaking there are ten thousand artists who would paint

The Embarcation for Cythera or the *Peasants Feast* or *St. Francis receiving the Stigmata* or Water or Air, Fire or anything, over again—strictly speaking there would be a difference but it would consist of such infinitesimally distinctive shades, of such an endless fractional scale of greatness that until further notice our feelings alone can assess that A note. For they may have rare colouring, or felicity in their layout or in the power of the composition, but they lack that air of greatness, that note of solemnity and lastly that eternal look which makes them inimitable and which is inexpressible. For the thing which decides and in the last analysis settles the question, is as much external to us as in the inexpressible. Beauty exists because we feel it, we know it, our lost friend, our child come home, our father revisited. The story lies forgotten (Meissonier and *La Rixe*, *The Cavaliers in the Forest*, *the Reader*, *The Trooper*, and the rest), not the subject of the painting but that frail look of heavenly truth, the pleasant branches, the saintly look on the faces, the precise cut of the trousers, perhaps anecdotal truth on the whole, as fleeting as a usurped reputation.

Greatness is eternal, the great dates of a man's life transposed into action, while the fleeting is anecdotal, even with an appearance of truth, but one which fades with the illusion of truth, surface truth, true one day no longer true the next, while art is today and still today tomorrow.

PICTORIAL VALUES AND THE LOUVRE

Above all, values have become a metaphysical question for us. We especially look for the main tenets on which works must be based, as well as those under whose influence all extant work must fall. We can throw some light on cubist art from the fact of cubist tendencies in poetry today.

These poets are unable to invent or find anything which could take its place in the repertoire of our hearts.

To make clear the division of our conscious states into

different unrelated levels, they compartmentalise, producing a mosaic of subconscious imagery in accordance with irrational disorder—and after all can it truly be said there is really any relation between them and weren't these states linked arbitrarily, as if they had engendered one another and does the conscious act in this way? I have similar concepts at times of most obvious mental disorder.

On the one side our judgement is tainted with sensual emotions (the somewhat rudimentary instruction of our senses) e.g. a cobbler experiences feelings of as deep and intense a nature in front of a Detaille as we in front of an Odilon Redon. (We know how the hour of the day influences us, the quality of the light, memories, sorrow, indigestion, the state of our humours. Is not the absolute only a norm?)

If the absolute exists of itself, then are we not justified in looking for art liberated from sensory conditioning, a new art which would accomplish a divorce between feeling and reason (a geometric art), which would only allow feelings of a pure intellectual order (are there any) which would not be indebted to contributions by the senses strictly speaking, in a word, our nerves within us.

Thus the manifestations of the art contained in the Louvre are only worth as much as the concepts on which they were founded, whose value is just what we are calling into question anew.

I will hasten to say standards are always necessary, that working to plan, following one line, we will never be able, even when faced with pure reason, to separate ourselves from a certain co-ordination, a certain readability. For, being human, we can only hypothetically create relations between planes and lines our senses could not recognise.

Finally, being unable to envisage anything sensible beyond the forms our senses offer our reason, we would certainly be forced to revert to painting and poetry for Everyman, but by sticking closer to the demands of reason.

THE PAINTER WHO BEST REPRESENTS THE NATIONAL GENIUS AND THE SCULPTOR

Where is the national genius to be found—is it in the initial inspiration, in the emotional curb, in the level of thought or simply sprung out of the ground, a certain lumping together of forms, tendencies and repulsions?

But for those who find Chardin stands for France and that Delacroix, for example, is an exception in France, there is no meeting point, except in a kind of incapability or lack of communication.

If I had to state who to my mind best represented what is customarily called native genius, I would say Watteau, as would most of my fellow citizens. For me, whoever says France says controversy, sterility, crystallisation, and obstacles. I did not say proportion, order, composition (see Poussin), I said *stratification.* Delacroix is French for me for this reason, not only because he represents, but because he *implies*, and is incapable of representing.

French art lacks true moral torment. I do not mean anxiety or sorrow. I mean focal, essential, absorbing torment. Disillusionment, yes, and even more, grief (although so little) but depth, questioning, or breaking, *never*! Externally drunk, Dionysiac as much as you like, and even on the edge of intoxication, a window on infinity, something between decay and phosphorous which Delacroix sometimes has.

But all this is still restricted, conscious, perfectly definable. No French painter ever gives us the feeling that his nature transcends him.

What characterises our own grace is that it is defined. Those portraits most full of spirituality, those most pregnant with psychological revelation, hardly reveal anything but a tangible, conscious level of the soul. I am thinking of Gustave Ricard and the portrait of his mother.

The heavy, bestial art Lucas Cranach offers us surely gives us more to think about with its solemn, distraught animalism than Prud'hon's nobler Art, for example.

I deliberately chose a *graceful* painter as his Art does not conflict. One of the characteristics of foreign artists is they seem racially motivated, while each French artist defines his own race and it seems, terminates it.

In this way we can put Fouquet, Clouet, Courbet and Corot jointly on the one side and Fragonard, Watteau, Latour and Prud'hon on the other. In the middle are Poussin and Le Nain.—Off to one side, David and Ingres whom I refuse to put with Poussin because of their great predictability.

I would therefore put the national geniuses which I see in a certain rigidity, a subconscious delimitation of thought, feeling and form (as against conscious rigidity, suppressing whole areas of thought and Protestant feeling in the person of Ingres, who included Grace, purity, psychology, and voluptuousness within the rigidity of a perfect form).

The problem seems to me easier in sculpture. I see the national spirit of French sculpture in a sort of mixture of grace and barbarousness. I am thinking of the Cathedrals, of the Virgins carved in wood. Rodin blends the barbarity of the delightful wood and stone carvers with grace and thought.

My favourite painter—Delacroix for the reasons given above. Because in substance he is least French.

An Actor.

CUP AND BALL

CUP AND BALL

There are not enough magazines, or if you prefer, all magazines are useless. We are going into print because we believe we are fulfilling a purpose. We are *real.* At a pinch, therefore, this excuses us from being necessary. There ought to be as many magazines as there are valid *states of mind.* The amount of printed paper would then be reduced to a minimum, but this minimum would provide a summary and the quintessence of what should be thought or what is worth publishing.

All magazines slavishly follow a *line of thinking*, and as a result they despise *thought.* They all make the serious mistake of being edited by several men. Thus while they fancy they reflect public feeling, they are only a hodge-podge. For there is no public feeling, there are various opinions which are more or less worth formulating. But humanity is incurable, no one will ever stop men being certain about their ideas and suspicious of those of others. And if someone who has a correct idea wants to make it known, he only has to start a magazine. We hold opinions which are worth expressing. Circumstances beyond thinking correctly or incorrectly prevent magazines from welcoming these absolutely bare-faced opinions. There are no free magazines, every magazine follows a creed more or less. Thus we have chosen the only way to be ourselves and to be so completely.

We will go into print when we have something to say. When we think we have found interesting views on an incorrect way of thinking, or if we consider an aesthetic or ethical question is susceptible to discussion. This magazine will therefore be a *personal* one, interesting in as much as it will be one man's creation, but we will invite contributions from artists and writers whose work seems to agree with our own state of mind, to illustrate it, or to tally with it in any way whatsoever.

ECSTASY

Silvery brazier, embers scooped out
By the music of its inner power,
Hollowed out embers, freed, a cortex
Busy delivering worlds.

Exhausting research into ego,
Insight that overreaches itself,
Oh! to unite the ice-pyre
With the mind that conceived it.

The old unfathomable quest
Flows out in delight,
Palpable voluptuousness, ecstasy,
At the true ringing crystal.

Oh! ink-black music, music,
Music of buried coals,
Soft, ponderous, freeing us
With its secret luminescence.

NOCTURNAL FEAST

This feast links the ponds
With the flashing stellar train,
With its cornucopias in which
Our brilliant dreams roll around.

It empties its soul waste
Somewhere between heaven and earth,
None in the burning night
Mistake them for flying swans.

And we, soft-spoken observers
Of the transformation of our bones,
Also see the stars of our
Exhilarating dreams dissolve.

We rarely write on the level of that automatism which governs the consummation of our thoughts.

The highest art consists in giving to the expression of thought, through the stratagems of well-applied rhetoric, in speech as well as in prose, the terseness and truth of its initial stratifications. And the art is, to return this rhetoric to the necessary point of precision, to make it one with certain real modes of existence in feeling and thought.—In a word, the only kind of writer who lasts is one who has been able to make such rhetoric behave as if it already came from thought, not just a thinking gesture. *Jean Paulhan*, who, in the *Bridge Crossed* defined how our thoughts behave in certain ways in relation to dreams, revealed such stratifications of human thought with infinitely more tact, aptness and sureness of touch than Maeterlinck did such contingencies of the soul—by far more submissiveness to the subject and by precise clarification of that subject.

RIMBAUD AND THE MODERNS

New events in thought, stimuli, enlivening relationships—not relationships between the feelings, between the inside of one feeling and the inside of another feeling, but a feeling's exterior, its place, its status, between the *importance* of another feeling and the external, metaphorical value of an idea in relation to another idea—and its reactions in relation to it, its recognition within him, its twists, its turns—this is Rimbaud's contribution.

Rimbaud taught us a new way of existing, of behaving in the midst of life.

Plundered by the moderns solely for his twists and turns, for the interplay of relationships invented by him and not even for the sort of thing he discussed—which incidentally he only treats externally (by feeling these externals on the surface) and if he digs down it is once again in order to bring out further externals. The inner essence of events always remained unknown to him—and the moderns have not even retained these phenomena, only ways of discussing them. Isn't this so Raval, Fierens and the other followers? Another mind is at the source of certain mannerisms of contemporary style, as quickly out of date as are all the affections of decadence, this source is Mallarmé in *Maunderings*.

The former, through his concern with giving each word its complete meaningful content, classified his words as values existing outside that thought which qualified them and affected those stranger inversions of syntax where each syllable seems to be embodied and to take on weight. But Mallarmé had to struggle with his thought while Fierens is only a struggle for his readers with an insignificant being for his subject. I hasten to say that Paul Fierens writes perfect little poems which seem to me like happy explanations of contemporary thought. I only object to his reviews.

A MIND PAINTER

In a foetal style *Paul Klee* (German) organises some interesting visions.

I quite like some of his nightmares, his mental syntheses conceived like architecture (or his architecture of a mental nature) and some cosmic syntheses where the entire secret objectivity of things is made perceptible, more than syntheses by *Georg Grosz*. Looked at side by side, the deep difference in their inspiration becomes apparent. *Georg Grosz* selects his world and brings it into his own vision; with *Paul Klee* the world's objects organise themselves—

and he only seems to compose at their dictation. The organisation of visions, forms, also fixing and stabilising ideas, pictorial induction and deduction, with the results stemming from them, also pictorial organisation, searching for the underlying meaning of a certain imagery and the clarification of mental visions. So this art seemed to me. Grosz's dryness and precision explodes before these organised visions, their visionary aspect remains, their nature as something mental.

THE RIVER OF FIRE

François Mauriac has just finished publishing a far-reaching, moral novel in the *N.R.F.*, and if it is true morals are the basis of our whole being and judge not only the quality but even more the solidity and value of our feelings, of a high literary standard. I think François Mauriac only really found himself starting with *The River of Fire*. For it is the first book where he succeeded in bringing his concentration, emotional powers and great sensitivity to bear on three or four sufficiently representative characters.

Catholicism is the wide-angle lens of his talent. It nourishes and deepens the source of his feelings, seasoned by a taste for sin. His preoccupation with sin, this sort of moral angle within which Mauriac obliges us to judge each of his characters' actions, bestows on these characters as well as on the unfolding of the environment they move about in, a noble human sense which probes into and sensitises their acts. Faced with their slightest impulses, the idea of a sin acts in relation to us, the readers, in the manner of a reagent. *The River of Fire* can be put side by side with Jacques Rivière's *Aimée*. There is the same gap separating these two books as there is between a surgical operation and the effusions of confession. Jacques Rivière seems to work on a sort of dead matter and each of its states seems fixed for ever. François Mauriac forgoes nothing of life, that sort of sentient attraction our actions have, the most abject of our soul's impulses, if we are willing to regard them on the level of the high principles which govern them.

MUSICIAN

Now your mask catches fire,
Musician, whose waxy veins
Light the hollow clowns
With your molten notes.

Lightning splits the bellies
Of the new ships you launch,
Build us a little hell
With your cavernous skies.

The stars you squander
The precious metals you create,
Make up the swift temple
Of our familiar feelings.

But now the loveliest church
Opens its deepest flutes,
Lovely church so often described,
Where only devils live.

SHACK

The organ had no midwife
But the shack crackled,
And my mother was the landlady
Where I became involved.

Doves of slender fire
Darted their fleecy flames,
On the specious bosom
Where dreams bound me down.

But later the bride split
The clear, canvas membrane
Where the narrow solar tent
Imprisons all our frolics.

LEVEL

Literature by the moderns cannot surpass the level which can be produced by a certain degree of intelligence allied to a favourable culture. It is even disturbing to see to what degree a certain ease of assimilation coupled to a sort of trickery, or precociousness proper to putrid periods, may take the place of talent and gives Messrs. Raval, Fierens, Crémieux and Morand a contraband literary existence. In matters of style, our era has only one originator, *Jean Giradoux*. The others are only plagiarists, superimpositors or mimics. The same elegance marks these others, the same good grooming, the same feeling of being up to date and knowing what is going on. What makes a poet is novelty (but genuine, compressed, spontaneous novelty) and at the same time the substance of his imagery, his emotional scale, the underground current—for the emotions certainly have a scale whose degrees indicate beauty. It would be wrong to think that exaltation (I do not mean the quality of the feelings, but their category, their level, their extent) cannot have degrees.

THE LITTLE NOVELIST

I have rarely read such a cynically silly novel as Raymond Radiguet's. All of man's apeish antics are to be found in it, like a telescoped maturation. If only Mr. Radiguet could throw overboard the youth he prides himself in wouldn't he do so! Yet it is his only charm: Raymond Radiguet excels in making use of that little dash of talent nature gave him. With remarkable precociousness he learned to isolate his talent from everything not his own. He learned to digest two hundred volumes and profit by them without this inconveniencing him in the least. None the less his material is too thin. His feelings are really those of a boy of seventeen and Mr. Radiguet is not so clever after all to make his meagreness appear inflated. The serious judgements which fall from his pen are always nicely ridiculous. Mr. Radiguet may do what he likes, he will never disguise his anaemic thought, arising from his extreme youth, this lack of solidity and density which Radiguet supplements with a certain inner tension everyone cannot possess, and of course one cannot replace experience.

The ability to say nothing of what should not be said, in a certain way makes up for sheer talent in Mr. Radiguet. It allows him to draw certain truthful images which set off his text. The pages on the mad-woman's capture are like the first draft of a type of direct literature where the very stuff of thought seems laid bare.

Thus this novel will never overlap any other. In certain ways it is a document.

Now Radiguet is dabbling in theatre criticism. The offhand manner with which this lad sometimes criticises people and a form which are beyond him has revealed the puffing up of his character and his ridiculous conceit in yet another way.

CONCERNING A POLEMIC

COCTEAU AND ALFRED POIZAT

Our sensibility has been given too many jolts to be moved for the sake of decency by certain conventionalised appearances, even material ones. What affects it rather than the nature and class of feelings, is its inner density, its force, its spark. We no longer believe in anything else. Greatness for its own sake is not greatness to us but the inner tension in things, their unquestionability. I think Cocteau has taken up *Antigone* in this sense. He went back to the original sources, the psychological sources, the human ones, not the literary sources—and also the mythological sources with the *real* drama they evoke. He wanted to give us a present-day equivalent to the essence of the old play, so we can believe in it anew. As to Poizat and his *Electra*, the flatness of his poetry, the bungling and tinsel insipidity of the production he is content with, proves his sorry concept of tragedy.

PAUL THE BIRDS
OR
THE PLACE OF LOVE
followed by
LETTER TO A LEMON-HEADED MAN

Paolo Uccello is busy thinking about himself, about himself and about love. What is love? What is the Mind? What is *My-self*.

Picture him as you like, standing, in front of a window or an easel or even without any sort of appearance, shorn of his body, as he would have liked to be. With nowhere in space to mark the location of his mind.

He is probing an inconceivable problem. To make up his mind as if it were not he who was making it up, seeing himself with his mind's eye, without it being his mind's eye. Retaining the benefit of his personal judgement by alienating the very individuality of that judgement. Seeing himself unaware it is he who sees himself. But this survey of himself should extend and take form before him like a measurable, composite landscape.

Yet as he continues to pursue this problem, it shifts. At times he is the container, at other times the contents. He is PRESENT, I mean present to us, to mankind in 1924 and he is himself. He is Paolo Uccello, he is his own myth as well, and he is becoming PAUL THE BIRDS.

(It is the same thing but it does not matter. By this I mean "Paolo Uccello" is his real, historic name, the one

THEY called him and "Paul the Birds" the one he hears us call him who are beyond time to him.)

Thus he builds up his own legend and little by little he is breaking away from himself. Replies criss-cross within him, outside time. And woe betide him if for one moment he averts his eyes from himself to savour his imposing tone. He is Paul the Birds. Did he not create this Selvaggia as *they* depict her or did she foist herself on him?

I am standing at the window, smoking. I am now Paul the Birds. The evening is fine, the sky towers. With each puff, the streets unwind with huge word-dwellings. Horns bellow. Gowns rend in the sky. All women are resolved in me. I am magnificent. The world is mine. Not the world. Just this tiny spot in the mind.

She is seated and she is dying. The fine myth, the fine design. To paint the vanishing of form, not the line which encircles all the others but the very one which is beginning not to exist.

Do you love me Selvaggia?

Yet it is true, I am not thinking of love. Meanwhile there is some love for me somewhere, near me. Where is the place of love?

My mind is a fiery number where the two ideas, love and the mind, meet. I gave up being a man a long time ago. I became her personal sacrifice. I was worthy of her unworldliness. Me, that is to say, one who was formerly Paolo Uccello, who let her die of hunger.

However, I saw her die. Donatello and Brunelleschi watched with me. I knew she was going to die, but her death only affected me mentally and here it is clearly no longer death. I am nearing the intangible line. MENTAL POEM.

Here we are. Brunelleschi is bawling me out.

We are discussing a detail about reality. (The point in question is Selvaggia's unworldliness as she, in short, is letting herself die for him, but she herself has no part in this unworldliness.)

ME—She came to me unconsciously.
She was unaware of her unworldliness.

And Paolo Uccello builds a whole fabric of illusory spirituality on the unconsciousness of this unworldliness. He puts her above life. There is unworldliness somewhere but not in her, since she is unaware of it. And I, Paolo Uccello, am also unworldly to her, and divorced from my own unworldliness. To which Brunelleschi quite rightly counters that she is alive and life alone permitted her to be unworldly. And you have killed life, Paolo Uccello, you disposed of life.

ME—I am the mind. The mind is above life.

BRUNELLESCHI—Oh! let us all die, let us do
away with all problems.
Let vain word-winds also fade away.
Each breath is empty.
The mind is not outside our lungs.
You, the Birds, are also flesh and
blood.

This touches me to the quick. I decline to give an opinion.

ME—I can't hear any more. I can't hear any more.

I am flesh and blood, of course I am flesh and blood. But I cannot see myself just now. I do not think of myself as being alive. I am such as I was made, that's all.

However, it is he who is building himself up. Besides you'll see. He goes on:

Yes, Brunelleschi, I am doing the thinking. Right now, you are speaking in me.

You are such as I would like to see you.

The discussion goes on at length . . . rapidly passing from one subject to the next. There comes a moment when Paolo Uccello is carrying on a great, lyrically preconceived tirade on the place of art in the mind. He says it in an incredibly faint voice like an old woman or a born idiot.

—The charnel house, you sculpted nothing but the charnel house. You have given falsehood a mask. You set falsehood up, liar, you defined falsehood in eternal time and the more liar you, as you did it in princely fashion.

(This is a first attempt at a mental drama.)

I saw this as a play, but it would take place solely in the mind. This is why I am so preoccupied about my character being physically real. Besides, do not look too far for the key to the piece. As I wrote I tried to carry out the same sort of mental operations on myself as I assigned to my characters. Hence the apparent confusion throughout. Or rather I attempted to fuse it with the myth of Paolo Uccello.

I am lodged in the myth.

I really am Paul the Birds.

My mind can no longer attempt the slightest deviation either left or right.

I am just as I saw myself.

This makes the play consistent.

At times I am in life and at other times I am above life. I am like a character in a play who has the power to look upon himself, being pure abstraction at times, simply a mental creation, and at other times the investor and animator of this man created in the mind. While being alive, he would then have the ability to deny his existence and escape his opponent's insistence, while the latter always stays as he is, all of a piece, from head to toe, and always seen from the same angle.

This is my superiority over Brunelleschi.

Yes, but what is the place of love in all this?

—It shares in the general unworldliness of Paolo Uccello's mind and perhaps brings him a little nourishment while being alive. It gives him the impulse to create. Another intangible point.

But let us go on delving into this problem.

In this way, therefore, Brunelleschi establishes his position by participating in life.

BRUNELLESCHI—I, Brunelleschi, have sculpted life.
I have given form to life's forms.
I have finished off landscapes.

No need to tell you Brunelleschi is in love with Paul the Birds' wife. Among other things he blames him for letting her starve to death (can one starve to death in the mind?).

To which Donatello, who is also present, retorts:

—You do not know the language of true love, Brunelleschi.

The discussion becomes a vast stage.

Let us therefore portray the characters and give them a physical appearance, a voice and costume.

Paul the Birds' voice is barely audible, he walks like an insect and his robe is too big for him.

Brunelleschi, on the other hand, has a real stage voice, deep and fruity. He looks like Dante.

Donatello is somewhere between the two: St. Francis of Assisi before the Stigmata.

The action takes place on three levels.

Imagine a cross-section through the mind and in opposition to it, things whirring. The mind arbitrarily becomes wedded to a theme, to an objective. This theme and these words call a for stability and resonance of their own. There is only one sound left in the mind. And I turn myself inside out in the Mind. I am obsessed by the theme of Paolo Uccello, a fleeting theme whose contradictions keep coming back and penetrate under my Mind. Yet I am myself. I have not lost my density. The Mind and I size one another up face to face. Scum of a Mind. I cannot settle down to one theme. The whole theme has passed into me. I must go down into the heart of me. I am gazing on my theme and me. The theme has become my mouthpiece. I invoke all life. The sky is beautiful, my wife is lovely, horns bellow in the streets. I feel the sky cracking down on me. But Paolo Uccello and his inconsistent problem are calling me. I need to fuse them within me, that's what life is, that's what life is about. All of life at every instant. Everything the Mind busies itself with, all levels, all tendencies, all qualities. The worst, the absurd, incapability and disappearance.

—Then (   )[1] does not concern us.

—Of course it concerns us. Everything that is real concerns us. The Treaty of Versailles concerns us, or the Edict of Nantes or the *Confessions of an Opium Eater*. You can take this as the (   )[1] by one of the Damned.

I break down at every turn, my branchings off are legion. Well then. The cosmic agony of an era does not come through these thin leaves, only the mental agony of a man and the divergence of his thought. Furthermore, we can make out a theme of a so-called literary sort and though it is little, a care for style and substantiated imagery. I have already stated that all levels and all qualities can be found there, all tendencies. It is like a cross-section of the mind with sudden fits of incapability, minutely recorded. *Yet the sensation is the same all over.*

What is important in such an attempt?

The exaggerated material should be true.

We can do anything in the mind, we can speak in any tone of voice, *even one which is unsuitable.* There is no supposedly literary tone, any more than there are themes which are not allowed. If I like I can speak in a normal conversational tone. But I can give up the effect right away. I can give up all impressions. *There is only one thing which makes art, and that is the tangibility of man's intentions.*

Consciousness makes truth.

THE EVOLUTION OF DECOR

We must disregard production and the theatre.

All great dramatists, the genre dramatists, thought outside the theatre.

Look at Aeschylus, Sophocles and Shakespeare.

In another scale of ideas, look at Racine, Corneille and Moliére. These either do away with, or just about do away with, outside sets. But they are forever probing the inner scene changes, the sort of perpetual comings and goings of the protagonists' souls.

[1] Word missing

Subservience to the author, abiding by the text, what a dismal practice! Every text has endless possibilities. The spirit, not the letter of the text! A script requires more than analysis and insight.

A sort of magnetic inter-communication must be re-established between the minds of the author and producer. The producer must even put his own logic and understanding to one side. Up to now, those who have claimed to rely exclusively on the text, have perhaps managed to rid themselves of the smug mimicry of certain traditions, but above all they have not been able to put the theatre and their own understanding to one side. They placed certain Moliérian or Odonian traditions with new traditions from Russia or elsewhere. And whereas they were seeking to get rid of the theatre, they were still forever thinking theatre. They arranged their productions using the stage, the scenery and actors.

They thought of each play in relation to the theatre. Re-theatricalise the theatre, such is their latest monstrous cry. Whereas theatre must be thrust back into life.

This does not mean the theatre should imitate life. As if we were only able to ape life. What we need is to rediscover *the life of the theatre* in all its freedom.

This life is wholly comprised in the texts by the great tragedians, when we hear them in all their colour, when we see their great range, their many levels, volume, outlook and special density.

But we lack a capacity for mysticism. What good is a producer who is not used to searching within himself, above all, and who would not know, if necessary, how to withdraw and get free from himself? Such strictness is essential. We can only rediscover the purity of our initial reactions by dint of purifying our minds and forgetting ourselves. We must learn to give every theatrical movement its indispensable human sense.

For the moment, let us first look for plays that are like a transubstantiation of life. We go to the theatre to escape ourselves, or if you rather, to discover not so much what is better, but what is more unusual and *selected* in ourselves.

Everything is allowed in the theatre except the *jejeune* and the "topical". Just look at painting. There are young painters just now who have rediscovered the meaning of real painting. They paint chess or card players who are like gods.

Why is our modern world so attracted by the circus and music hall? I would willingly use the word fantasy if I did not feel it so debased, at least as we understand it today, and if it did not result in research dealing only with the *re-theatricalisation* which is the latest rage, the contemporary ideal. No, I prefer to say we must intellectualise the theatre and put the feelings and actions of the characters on a level where they have a more vital and unusual meaning. The theatre must be made more subtle in mood. This does not involve any very lofty metaphysical process. The circus is a proof of this. Simply the meaning of mental values. This would do away with, or put at least three-quarters of current productions outside the theatre, but it would both save the theatre and make it return to its source. To save the theatre I would even get rid of Ibsen because his protagonists discuss points of philosophy or morals which do not sufficiently affect their souls *in relation to us*.

Sophocles, Aeschylus and Shakespeare covered up certain pangs of the soul that were a little too pedestrian by that sort of holy terror which weighed down on the actions of their heroes and to which, after all, audiences were more sensitive to than today.

What we have lost on the strictly mystical side we can make up on the intellectual side.

But to do this, we must learn to be mystics once again, at least in a certain sense, by concentrating on the lines, forgetting ourselves, forgetting the theatre, waiting for and determining the ideas born within us, naked, natural and exaggerated, and to see these ideas through to the end.

To get rid, not only of all reality, all verisimilitude, but even all logic, if we can still glimpse life at the end of such illogicality.

In practice, and since after all we need rules, here are a few concrete ideas:

It is certain everything obviously false in the theatre contributes to creating the mistake we are suffering from. Look at clowns. They build up a scene by the way they level a glance. Thus there is only reality on stage. But this has all been said before. People won't stand three dimensional actors moving in front of flats, their faces a painted mask. There is no illusion, even in the front row of the stalls. Either the stage needs to be moved back or we must get rid of the entire visual part of the show.

Furthermore, in order to render us more sensitive to various mental levels, we must set up a sort of physical bridge between Shakespeare and ourselves. Any actor whose costume puts him outside everyday life without casting him in the part, might as well be watching the play without taking part in it. A sort of character in a top-hat, without any make-up, who would stand out from the company by his bearing. The structure of the theatre would have to be changed so the stage could be moved according to the requirements of the action. The strictly spectacular side of plays would likewise have to be dropped. Then one would go there not so much to see, as to take part.

The audience should get the feeling they can do what the actors are doing without much technical knowledge.

Given these few rules, the rest depends on the producer's creativity and he must find the elements of suggestion and style, the requisite line and designs most suitable to conjure up the work's own mood and illusion.

In the light of the brain's evidence and reality,

at the point where the world grows loud and strong in us,

with the eyes of a man who feels things rebuilding within him and who fastens on to and becomes set on the start of a new reality.

Those states of mind where the simplest, the most

commonplace reality does not reach me, where the instant pressure of habitual reality does not come through to me and I do not even attain the necessary bare subsistence level.

Let this pressure and this feeling within you appear to the world with their evidence and normal density, in accordance with your being in a system, with a given amount that represents you, with *the given amount* that represents you.

Not strictly speaking the volume of things, but their feeling and resonance within me. The resonance which results in thought.

To get carried away by things instead of fixing on one of their specious aspects, endlessly searching for definitions which only reveal their lesser aspects,

but to do that, to have the current of things in you, to be on a level with that current, at least to be level with life, instead of our deplorable mental state continually leaving us between two stools,

to be on a level with objects and things, having both their global form and meaning within us,

that both the locations of your thinking matter and the feeling and vision of them within you should start moving at the same time,

*

Once and for all

1. I certainly seem horribly concerned with showing I do not think and realise I have a feeble mind but first, I believe all men have feeble minds—and second, that it is better to be weak, it is better to be in a continual state of abdication towards our minds. It is a fitter state for man, a more normal state, better adapted to our fatal condition as men, to man's fatal claim to will.

My imagination is deadened.

*

Mountains of problems hem us in on all sides. Woe unto he who thinks he can escape them, woe unto he who imagined he could do without thought.

What era contains, can show to its credit, this desperate effort at conquest situated on the icy summits of the Mind.

ON SUICIDE

Before committing suicide, I would like to be given some real assurance of being. I would like to be sure about death. Life appears to me merely as consent to the apparent legibility of things and their coherence in the mind. I no longer feel like the irreducible crossroads of things; death the healer heals by severing us from nature. Yet what if I an only a sink full of pain things do not flow out of?

If I kill myself, it won't be to destroy myself, but to rebuild myself. For me, suicide would only be a means of violently reconquering myself, of brutally invading my being, of anticipating God's unpredictable approach. I would reintroduce my designs into nature through suicide. For the first time I would give things the shape of my will. I would free myself from the conditioned reflexes of my organs which are so badly correlated with my ego. Then life would not just be an absurd accident—where I think what I am told to think—then I would select my thought and the direction of my faculties, tendencies and reality. I would put myself half-way between beauty and ugliness, good and evil. I would put myself in suspension, without any inclinations, neutral, poised between good and evil temptations.

For life is no solution in itself, life has no sort of chosen, accepted or self-determined existence. It is just a series of desires and opposing forces, petty contradictions which succeed or miscarry according to the circumstances of detestable chance. Evil, like genius and madness, is unequally apportioned in all men. Good, like evil, is a product of circumstances and a more or less active catalyst.

It is certainly abject to be created and live and sense yourself irrevocably predestined in the darkest corners of your mind, down to the most *unthought of* ramifications of your being. After all, we are only trees and it is probably written somewhere in some crook of my family tree that I will kill myself on a given day.

The very concept of freedom to commit suicide falls like a cut-down tree. I create neither the time nor the place nor the circumstances of my suicide. I did not even invent the idea of it, would I feel it when it uproots me?

It may be that at that moment my being will dissolve, but if it remained whole, how would my damaged organs react? With what non-existent organs would I register the laceration of this suicide?

I feel death sweep over me like a torrent, like an instantaneous flow of lightning whose charge I cannot envisage. I feel death laden with pleasures, and whirling labyrinths. Where is the idea of myself in all this?

But suddenly God appeared like a fist, like a scythe of cutting light. I voluntarily cut myself off from life, I wanted to stem the tide of my fate!

This God has disposed of me to the point of absurdity. He kept me alive in a void of denials and furious self-disavowals. He destroyed everything in me, right down to the last surge of my conscious, sentient life. He reduced me to a walking automaton, but an automaton who feels the rupture of his unconscious self.

And thus I wanted to prove I was alive, I wanted to get back in touch with the resonant reality of things, I wanted to break with my fate.

And what did God say to that?

I had no feeling of life, and the flow of all moral concepts was like a dry river in my veins. Life was not an object or form to me, it had become a series of rationalisations. But these rationalisations never got off the ground and only freewheeled, they were like possible "diagrams" within me which my will-power could not light on.

Even to arrive at this suicidal state, I must wait for my ego to return, I need the free play of all the articulations of my being. God set me down in despair as in a constellation of stalemates whose radiance terminates in me. I can neither live nor die, but am unable not to wish to live or die. And all men are like me.

THE BAD DREAMER

My dreams are mostly a liquid. I am immersed in sorts of nauseous waters where blood-red films toss and turn. I never rise up to the level of certain impressions, whether in my dreams or in real life. I am never settled in the continuity of my life. My dreams are offered no escape, no refuge or guide. Truly the rankness of severed limbs.

Besides, I am too resigned about my thought to be interested in anything that goes on in it. I ask for one thing only: to be locked away in my thought for good.

And as to the physical appearance of my dreams, I told you, a liquid.

THE TREE

This tree and its rustling
Forest dark with calls,
With cries,
Consumes the night's dark heart.

Vinegar and milk, sky, ocean,
The sky's dense mass,
Everything conspires towards this quivering
Lying in the dense heart of darkness.

A bursting heart, a solid star,
Divides and melts in the sky;
The limpid sky splits open,

At the ringing sun's call,
Making the same sound, making the same sound
As night and trees in the eye of the storm.

THE STREET

The sexual street comes to life
Along the ill-shaped fronts,
The cafés, chirping with crimes,
Uproot the avenues.

Sex's hands burn their pockets
While their bellies seethe down below;
The thoughts all clash,
The heads less than the holes.

NIGHT WORKS

Deep down in the swollen sheets
Where the whole night breathes,
The poet feels his hair
Proliferate and grow.

Uprooted glasses pile up
On all the world's bars,
The poet feels his thoughts
And his genitals desert him.

For here life and the womb
Of thought are on trial,
Bottles strike the heads
Of the Aerial gathering.

The Word grows out of sleep
like a flower or a glass
Full of forms and fumes.

The glasses and bellies collide
Life is transparent
In the crystal heads.

The poet's fiery aeropagitica
Gathers about the green carpet;
The void spins.

Life crosses the mind
Of the thick-haired poet.

In the street only a window,
Cards flap;
In the window the vaginal woman
Places her belly under consideration.

SOUND PANES

Sound panes where stars turn
Glasses where brains stew
The Heavens teeming with affrontery
Devour the stars in their nakedness.

An odd, violent milk
Teems in the bowels of the firmament;
A snail climbs and disturbs
The serenity of the clouds.

Delights and furies, the whole sky
Showers a whirlwind of wild wings,
Sweltering obscenities
Over us, like a cloud.

NIGHT

The buses run through the gutters
Rain drifts up to the moon,
In the avenue a window
Discloses a naked woman.

The obtuse ceiling's face
Views the resting bodies,
Life is a complete meal
Between the cobbles and the sky.

Poet, those things preying on your mind
Have nothing to do with the moon,
The rain is cool
The belly good.

Deep down in the swollen sheets
Where the whole night breathes,
The poet feels his hair
Proliferate and grow.

See how glasses pile up
On all the world's bars,
Life is empty
Minds are far away.

Somewhere a poet is thinking.
We do not need the moon,
The mind is wide,
The world is full.

People tremble
In each room
Life brings forth something
Which drifts to the ceiling.

A pack of cards floats in the air
Around the glasses.
Wine fumes, glasses fume
And the evening's pipes.

The maritime fumes
Of ill-constructed dreams,
Collect in slanting ceiling corners
Of all the trembling rooms.

For here life and the womb
Of thought are on trial,
Bottles strike the heads
Of the aerial gathering.

The Word grows out of sleep
Like a flower or a glass
Full of forms and fumes.

The glass and belly collide
Life is transparent
In the crystal-clear heads.

The poets' fiery aeropagitica
Gathers about the green carpet.
The void spins.
Life crosses the mind
Of the thick-haired poet.

In the street only a window,
Cards flap.
In the window the vaginal woman
Places her belly under consideration.

LOVE WITHOUT A TRUCE

This thirsting water triangle,
This unsignposted way
Madam, and the signs from your masts
On this, my drowning sea.

The signals from your hair
The shot from your lips.
This storm carrying me away
In the wake of your eyes.

Finally this shadow, on the shore
Where life holds a truce, and the wind,
And the awful trampling
Of the crowd on the way.

When I raise my eyes towards you
The world seems to tremble,
And the fires of love are like
Your husband's caresses.

THE CHAINED MUMMY

Grope at the door, eyes dead,
Turned inwards on this corpse
This scorched corpse washed
By your body's hideous silence.

The gold which rises, the intense
Silence cast on your body
And the tree you still bear
And that dead man walking forward.

—This is how the spindles turn
In the fibres of the scarlet heart
This great heart where the sky explodes
While gold submerges your bones.—

The harsh background landscape
Reveals itself as you walk,
And eternity overtakes you
For you cannot cross over.

THE SITUATION OF THE FLESH

I am reflecting on life. All the systems I could devise would never equal these cries by a man occupied in rebuilding his life.

I can conceive a system in which the whole man would be involved, man with his physical body and the summits, the intellectual projection of his mind.

It seems to me one must above all reckon with man's incomprehensible magnetism and with what, for want of a more telling phrase, I am forced to call his life-force.

My reason will certainly one day have to receive these unformulated forces exteriorly shaped like a cry which are besieging me, and they may then supplant higher thought. There are intellectual cries, cries which stem from the marrow's *delicacy*. This is what I personally call the Flesh. I do not separate my thought from my life. With each of my tongue's vibrations I retrace all the paths of my thought through my flesh.

One must have been deprived of life, of the nervous irradiation of existence, of the conscious fulfilment of our nerves, to realise to what extent the Sensation and Knowledge of all thought is secreted in the nervous energy within our bones. Also how mistaken are those who bank on intelligence and pure intellect. Above all, there is the completeness of the nerves. Completeness which contains all consciousness and the magic ways of the mind through the flesh.

But what am I in the midst of this theory about the Flesh or more correctly, Existence? I am a man who has lost his life and who is seeking every way of re-integrating it in its proper place. In some measure I am the Generator of my own vitality. Vitality which is more precious to me than consciousness, for what in other men is only the means of being Human is all of Reason to me.

In the course of this research buried in the limbo of my consciousness, I thought I felt explosions, like the shock of magic stones or the sudden petrification of fires. Fires like imperceptible truths, miraculously vitalised.

But one must walk slowly along the road of dead stones, especially someone who has lost his *understanding of words*. It is this indescribable knowledge which explodes in gradual thrusts. And whoever possesses it does not understand it. But the Angels also do not understand, for all real knowledge is *obscure*. Clear Mind is a property of matter, I mean the Mind, at a given moment, is clear.

But I must look into this aspect of the flesh which is supposed to give me a metaphysics of Being and a positive understanding of Life.

For me, whoever says Flesh says *apprehension* above all, hair standing on end, flesh exposed, with all the intellectual depth of this show of pure flesh and all its sensory consequences, that is, feeling.

Whoever says feeling also says intuition, that is, direct knowledge, inverted communications enlightened from within. There is a mind in the flesh, but a mind as quick as lightning. And yet the agitation of the flesh partakes of the mind's higher matter.

Yet whoever says flesh also says sensibility. Sensibility, that is, assimilation, but an intimate, secret, profound, total, assimilation of my own pain and as a result sole, unique knowledge of this pain.

MANIFESTO IN PLAIN TERMS

To Roger Vitrac

If I believe neither in Good nor Evil, if I feel so destructively predisposed, if there is nothing I can readily agree to concerning first principles, the principle of this is in my bones.

*

I am destructive because to me, everything arising from reason does not hold together. Now, I only believe in the evidence of whatever excites my nerves, not what is addressed to my reason. I have discovered levels in the nervous field. I now feel able to decide on the evidence. For me this proof is in the realm of the flesh itself but it has no connection with the evidence of reason. The eternal war between heart and mind is decided in the flesh itself, but in my flesh irrigated by my nerves. In the field of emotional intangibles, the impressions conveyed by my nerves assume the form of the highest intellectuality and I refuse to strip them of their intellectual nature. In this way I watch a concept taking shape which contains the lightning in things themselves and bears down on me with a noise like genesis. No imagery satisfies me unless it is also

Knowledge, unless it bears its own substance as well as its own clarity. My mind, being tired of discursive reasoning, wants to be carried away by the mechanics of a new, total gravitation. For me, it is like that sovereign reorganisation in which only illogical laws play a part and where the discovery of a new Sense is triumphant. This Sense lost in the confusion of drugs which, in sleep, gives contradictory illusions the appearance of profound intelligence. This Sense is the mind conquering itself and although irreducible by reasoning, exists, but only *within the mind*. It is order, intellect, the meaning of chaos. But it does not accept chaos just as it is. It interprets it and by so doing, loses it. It is the logic of Illogic. I need say no more. My lucid irrationality does not fear chaos.

*

I renounce nothing which is Mind. I simply want to transfer my mind, its laws and organs, elsewhere. I do not give myself up to the mind's sexual automatism but, on the contrary, am seeking to isolate the discoveries which explicit reason does not give me, out of this very automatism. I give myself up to feverish dreams, but I do so in order to deduce new laws. In delirium, I seek multiplicity, subtlety and the eye of reason, not rash prophecies. There is a knife-edge here I cannot forget.

*

But it is a knife-edge midway through dreams. I keep it within me and I do not allow it to advance to the borders of the clear senses.

*

Whatever is part of the realm of images cannot be broken down by reason and must remain images under penalty of destroying themselves.

However, there is reason in the images, there are clearer images in the world of graphic vitality.

Multiform glittering microbes are injected into the urgent teeming of the mind. This insentient, *thinking* dust-haze is regulated in accordance with the laws it deduces from itself, on the borders of lucid reasoning and consciousness, or reason *cut across.*

*

True illusion, material error, does not exist in the heightened field of the imagination, but the illusions of knowledge exist all the more. And all the more so the feeling of new knowledge can and must extend into real life.

The truth of life lies in the impulsiveness of matter. Man's mind is in disorder in the midst of concepts. Do not expect man to be content, just expect him to remain calm, to believe he has found his rightful place. For only Madmen are really calm.

THE MUMMY CORRESPONDENCE

This body which is no longer contiguous with life,

this tongue, no longer able to force its way out of its shell,

this voice no longer travels the road of sound,

this hand has forgotten more than how to grip, and is no longer able to gauge the distance in which to accomplish its grip,

finally this brain where ideas are no longer decided along its lines,

all this which makes up my fresh-bodied mummy, gives God a glimpse of the void into which being born necessarily put me.

Neither is my life complete, but nor have I completely aborted death.

Physically I do not exist, owing to this massacred, incomplete body, no longer able to nourish my thoughts.

I am destroying myself mentally, I no longer admit I am alive. My sensitivity is on a level with the stones, little short of worms or the vermin of abandoned tips crawling out of it.

But this death is much more rarified, this multiple death

of myself comes from a sort of rarification of my flesh. My intellect is bloodless. The nightmare squid shoots out all its ink, clogging the mind's outlets, and this blood has even lost its veins, the flesh being insensitive to the knife edge.

Essential fire still circulates from top to bottom of this furrowed, uncompacted flesh. Lucidity hourly kindles the fire's coals, uniting life and its flowers.

Everything which has a name under the heavens' compact vault, everything which has features—which is the vital centre of breath and the ligament of tremors, all of this passes into the spirals of this fire where the flesh's very waves curl back, this flaccid, hard flesh rising up one day like a deluge of blood.

Have you seen the mummy stark and stiff at the intersection of phenomena, this ignorant, living mummy, ignorant as to all the limits of its emptiness, panic-stricken by the throbbing of its death.

The voluntary mummy is raised up, and all reality moves around it. And consciousness, like a fire-brand, runs through the entire field of its compelled virtuality.

There is bodily loss in this mummy, and there is complete incapability to conjure up this body in the melancholy speech of its intellectual flesh. This feeling running through the veins of this mystical body, in which each convulsion is a manner of world and another sort of birth, loses and consumes itself in the burning of mistaken oblivion.

Oh! to be the foster-father of this suspicion, the multiplier of such engendering and this world in its pleasures, in its flowering consequences.

But this flesh is only the beginning and only abstraction, abstraction. . . .

Abstraction.

SURREALIST TEXT

The physical world was still there. My ego's rampart

watched, where an ochre red fish had been washed up, made of dry air, coagulated, drained off water.

But something had suddenly happened.

A shattering arborescence and threadbare, shiny brows reflected, with something like a perfect navel, but indistinct, the colour of blood diluted with water, and in front of it, a grenade which also shed blood mixed with water, which scattered blood with lines dripping down. And in these lines, breast-circles drawn in the brain's blood.

But the air was like an exhausting vacuum in which this woman's bust was drawn up in the general quaking, the shaking of this glassy world, slewed about in frontal explosions, shook its columnary vegetation, its nest of eggs, its spiral knots, its mental mountains and its surprised façades. And suns caught at random in the columnary façades, suns like eggs, erect on air jets, and my brows brushed aside the columns, the fleecy air, the solar mirrors, the new-born spirals, towards the precious bustlines, the navel hollow and the non-existent belly.

But all the columns lose their eggs and, breaking the line of columns, ovary eggs were born, eggs like turned over vaginas.

The mountain is dead, the air is eternally dead. In this crucial world breakup, all sounds are trapped in ice, movement is trapped in ice. And my brow's efforts have frozen.

But under the ice a frightening noise shot through with fire cocoons enfolds the silence of the naked belly deprived of ice, and turned-over suns rise looking at one another, black moons, terrestrial fires and milk waterspouts.

The columns coldly swaying, divided my mind two ways and I touched my own genitals, the organs at the base of my soul, which rose in a glowing triangle.[1]

INQUIRY

WE LIVE, WE DIE, WHAT IS THE ROLE OF FREE WILL IN

[1] This text was written under the inspiration of Mr. André Masson's paintings.

ALL THIS? IT SEEMS PEOPLE KILL THEMSELVES IN THE SAME WAY AS THEY DREAM. THIS IS NOT A MORAL QUESTION WE ARE ASKING:

IS SUICIDE A SOLUTION?

No, suicide is still a hypothesis. I claim the right to question suicide, just as I question the whole of the rest of reality. For now, and until some future date, *we must* be terribly doubtful, not only about existence, strictly speaking, which anyone can grasp, but about the inner agitation and deep sensitivity in things, actions and reality. I believe in nothing to which I am not joined by the sensitivity of a thinking, meteor-like, umbilical cord. All the same, I am a little short of active meteorites. All mankind's sentient blueprints of existence bother me and I resolutely loathe all reality. Suicide is no more than the distant, legendary conquest of clear-thinking men, but strictly speaking, I find a suicidal state incomprehensive. A neurasthenic's suicide represents no consequences whatsoever, as against the state of the soul of a man who has really planned his suicide, the material circumstances and the moment of wonderful release. I have no idea what things really are, or of any human state of mind, nothing in this world runs true for me or runs true in me. Life makes me suffer terribly. I cannot attain any existing state of mind. And I most certainly died a long time ago, my suicide has already taken place. That is, my inner self has been killed. But what would you think of a *prior suicide*, a suicide which would make us retrace our steps, but on the other side of existence, not on the side of death. That is the only one which has any meaning to me, I feel no longing for death, I feel a longing *not to be*, never to have fallen into this sink of imbecilities, abdications, renunciations, and obtuse contacts which are Antonin Artaud's ego and much weaker than him. The ego of this wandering invalid who, from time to time comes to exhibit his shadow he himself spat on long ago, this hobbling, limping self, this virtual, impossible ego which none the less finds itself in real life. No one like him has ever felt his weakness which is mankind's most important, basic weakness. To destroy, not to exist.

GENERAL SECURITY
THE LIQUIDATION OF OPIUM

My intention is plain: I mean to exhaust this question, then they can stop needling us about the supposed danger of drugs for good.

My point of view is distinctly anti-social.

There is only one reason to attack opium. It is the fear its use may become general throughout society.

Now this danger is false.

We are born rotten in body and soul, we are congenitally unfit. Suppress opium and you are not going to suppress the need for crime, the cankers of body and soul, an inclination to despair, born cretinism, hereditary syphilis and the friability of instinct. You will never stop certain souls being destined for any sort of poison: morphine poisoning, compulsive poisoning, loneliness poisoning, *XX* poisoning, compulsive reading poisoning, loneliness poisoning, masturbation poisoning, repeated coitus poisoning, the soul's deep-rooted weakness poisoning, alcohol poisoning, tobacco poisoning, and anti-social poisoning. There are souls which are incurable and lost to the rest of society. Take one means of madness away from them and they will invent ten thousand others. They will create subtler, wilder, absolutely *desperate* means. Nature itself has an anti-social soul and it is only by usurping power that the organised body of society reacts against mankind's *natural* inclinations.

Let the lost lose themselves. We have better things to do with our time than to attempt to rehabilitate the unreformable and furthermore, this is useles, *abhorrent and harmful.*

As long as we have been unable to take away any reasons for human despair, we will never have the right to try and take away the means by which men try to cleanse themselves of despair.

For we would first have to suppress this natural hidden impulse, man's *plausible* bent which leads him to finding a way, giving him the *idea* of finding a way to extricate himself from his difficulties.

Furthermore, the lost are by nature lost and any ideas of moral reform will never do any good, *innate determinism exists*, there is an undoubted incurability about crime and suicide, imbecility and madness. There is an ungovernable cuckoldry in man, natural friability and castration of the mind.

Aphasia exists, *tabes dorsalis* exists, as do syphilitic meningitis, robbery and usurpation. Hell is already in this world and there are some men who are unhappy escapees from hell, escapees fated to repeat their escape *eternally*. Enough about that.

Man is wretched, the soul is weak, there are men who will always become lost. The means whereby they lose themselves matters little. *It is not society's business.*

We have clearly shown, have we not, that it can do nothing, it is wasting its time, and it should not insist on being rooted in its own stupidity,

In short, it is *harmful.*

For those who dare face the truth, we know, don't we, about the results of alcohol being prohibited in the United States.

A superproduction of madness. Beer on a diet of ether, alcohol laced with cocaine, sold under the counter, increased drunkenness, a sort of general intoxication. *In short, the law of the forbidden fruit.*

The same with opium.

This proscription increased curiosity about drugs and profited no one up to now except medical, journalistic and literary pimps. There are men who have built up busy, fecal reputations out of their supposed indignation against the tiny, inoffensive group of those damned by drugs (inoffensive because so few and always the exception), this minority, damned by their minds, their souls and their sickness.

Oh! how the umbilical cord of morality is tied tight in them. Since leaving their mothers, they have never sinned, have they. They are apostles, they are descendants of the pastors. We can only wonder where they get their indignation from, and especially how much they pocketed and in any case where did it get them.

Besides, that is not the point.

In fact, this furore against drugs and the stupid laws they result in:

1. *Is ineffectual against the need for drugs* which, sated or not, is innate to the soul and would induce it to resolutely anti-social acts, *even if drugs did not exist.*
2. *Aggravates the social need for drugs* and changes it into a secret vice.
3. *Is harmful to the true sickness*, for this is the real problem, the vital centre, the danger spot.

Unfortunately for sickness, medicine exists.

All the laws, all the restrictions, all the campaigns against narcotics will only amount to taking away the solvent of their ills, nourishment more wonderful than bread to them, and finally the means to re-enter life, from all those in need through human pain, who have an inalienable claim on society.

Better the plague than morphine, cry state medics, better hell than life. Only idiots like J.-P. Liausu (who furthermore is an ignorant freak) claim we should *let the sick mortify in their own sickness.*

And this is where all the boorishness of these eminent people shows its hand and gives itself free reign: *in the name, it claims, of the general good.*

Commit suicide, desperate men, and you, tormented in body and soul, abandon all hope. There is no longer any solace for you in this world. The world lives off your charnel-houses.

And you, clear-sighted madmen, tabetics, cancer victims, chronic meningitis cases, no one understands you. You have a point within you which no doctor will ever understand and this is the spot which, to me, saves you and makes you majestic, pure and wonderful. You are outside life, you are above life, you suffer pain ordinary men do not know. You go beyond the normal level and this is why men bear a grudge against you. You poison their peace of mind, you make their stability evaporate. You suffer uncontrollable pain whose intrinsic nature is to be unadaptable to any known condition, unadaptable to words. You suffer repeated, fleeting pains, insoluble pains. Pain beyond thought, pain which is neither in body nor soul, *but which belongs to both.* And I share in your sickness and I ask you: who would dare to ration our tranquilisers? In the name of what higher clearness of mind, soul of our souls, we who are at the root of knowledge and lucidity. And this comes from our insistence, our persistence in suffering. We whom pain has caused to journey into our souls in search of a calm place to anchor, in search of stability in evil like others in good. We are not mad, we are wonderful healers, we know the right dose for souls, for sensibility, for our bones and our thought. We must be left alone, the sick must be left alone, we ask nothing of mankind, we only ask them to alleviate our pain. We have evaluated our lives well, when confronted by others and particularly confronted by ourselves we know what restrictions they comprise. We know what willing decay, what self-denials, what paralysis of subtleness our sickness forces us to undergo every day. We won't commit suicide right away. In the meantime, leave us alone.

1 January 1925

DINNER IS SERVED

Abandon the caverns of existence. Come, the spirit breathes outside the spirit. It is time to leave home. Surrender to Universal Thought. The Marvellous is at the root of the spirit.

We come from within the mind, from inside the brain. Ideas, logic, order, Truth (with a capital T), Reason; we bequeath all to the void of death. Beware of your logic, Gentlemen, beware of your logic. You do not know how far our hatred of logic can lead us.

Only in turning away from life, by checking the spirit, can the supposedly real physiognomy of life be determined, but reality is not to be found there. That is why you must not trouble our minds, we who aspire to a certain Surreal eternity and who for a long time now have not considered ourselves in the present, we who appear to ourselves as actual shadows.

Whoever judges us is unborn to the mind, we mean to that mind which for us is outside what you call mind. Our attention must not be too drawn to the chains that bind us to the mind's petrifying imbecility. We have laid our hands on a new sort of animal. The heavens respond to our attitude of wild absurdity. That habit you have of ignoring questions will not prevent the heavens opening up on the appointed day and establishing a new language in the midst of your imbecilic deals. We mean the imbecilic deals in your ideas.

There are omens in thought. Our attitude of absurdity and death is the most receptive. A wilfully sibylline world speaks through the gaps in a henceforth unviable reality.

*

Yes, this is now the only use language can henceforth have, a means to madness, eliminating thought, breakdowns, a maze of irrationalities, not a DICTIONARY into which such and such boars on the banks of the Seine channel their narrowing minds.

DREAM

I

This was an aerial film. From high up in a static airplane they were filming a machine taking off, a precision machine which knew just what it was doing. The air was filled with droning, as monumental as the light which filled it. But the searchlight sometimes missed the plane.

In the end, there were only two or three of us left on the plane's wings. The airplane hung from the sky. I felt sickened, balanced as I was. But as the machine rolled over we had to turn over in space, regaining our balance with the help of rings. The manoeuvre finally succeeded but my friends were gone. Only the mechanics remained, making their crankshafts turn in space.

At that moment one of the two wires snapped.

"Stop the works," I shouted to them, "I am falling!"

We were two thousand feet up.

"Take it easy," they answered, "you were born to fall."

We had to avoid walking on the craft's wings. Yet they felt quite strong under me.

And I yelled, "Because if I fall, I know I can't fly."

Then I felt everything crack up.

A shout, "Send out the scalpers."

And immediately I *imagined* that my legs were caught by the lariat's razor lash, the plane left my feet and left me hanging in the air, my feet on the ceiling.

I never knew if *it had happened.*

II

Then I immediately arrived at the expected matrimonial ceremony. Only virgins were getting married at this wedding, but there were also actresses and prostitutes. and to arrive at the virgin, you had to cross a little Amazon, a stream thick with rushes. Then the husbands locked themselves in with the virgins and embarked on them right away.

One among them, more of a virgin than the others, wore a dress with light checks. She had curly hair. She was possessed by a well-known actor and was short and quite plump. I was sorry she did not love me.

The door of the room they had put her in did not shut properly and through the crack in the door I watched her wantonness. Besides, I was fairly far from the crack, but of all those in the room, I was the only one who paid any attention to what was going on in the bedroom. She was already standing, naked, and I admired how immodesty clothed her in freshness and a sort of resolute determination. She had a clear feeling of her sex, but as something completely natural and normal at that moment. She was with her young husband. And thus we pursued them by boat.

III

There were three of us in monk's robes, and in the train of the monk's robes, Max Jacob showed up in a short coat. He wanted to reconcile me to life, either to life or himself, and before me I felt the dead weight of his reasoning.

We had previously been running a few women to earth. We possessed them on tables, over chairs, on the stairs, and my sister was one of them.

The walls were black, the doors stood out clearly and allowed vaulted lighting to shine through. The entire setting was a willed, *created analogy*. My sister lay on a table, already swollen and covered with coats. Only she was on another level than me, in another sphere.

There were transparent tables, doors and stairs. I felt all this was ugly. And we had to put on long robes to hide our sins.

Now my mother arrived dressed as an Abbess. I was afraid she would show up. But Max Jacob's short coat clearly indicated he had nothing left to hide.

He had two coats on, one green, the other yellow, and the green one was longer than the yellow. They appeared one under the other. We checked our credentials.

LETTER TO THE CHANCELLORS OF THE EUROPEAN UNIVERSITIES

Gentlemen,

In the narrow tank you call "Thought", the mind's

rays rot like old straw.

Enough playing on words, syntactic stratagems and formula-juggling. We must now discover the Heart's great Law, the Law which is not a Law (a prison) but a guide for the Mind lost in its own labyrinth. Further away than anything science will ever reach, where reason's rays break against the clouds, this labyrinth exists, a focal point where all the forces of being and the ultimate Spiritual veins converge. In this maze of moving and ever-changing walls outside all known forms of thought, our Spirit stirs, watching for its most secret and spontaneous movements—those with the character of a revelation, an air of having come from elsewhere, of having fallen from the sky.

But the race of prophets is extinct. Europe is becoming set in its ways, slowly embalming itself beneath the wrappings of its borders, its factories, its law-courts and its universities. The frozen Mind cracks between the mineral staves which close upon it. The fault lies with your mouldy systems, your logic of $2 + 2 = 4$. The fault lies with you, Chancellors, caught in the net of syllogisms. You manufacture engineers, magistrates, doctors, who know nothing of the true mysteries of the body or the cosmic laws of existence. False scholars blind outside this world, philosophers who pretend to reconstruct the mind. The least act of spontaneous creation is a more complex and revealing world than any metaphysics.

So leave us alone, Gentlemen, you are only usurpers. By what right do you claim to channel human intelligence and award certificates of Mental merit? You know nothing of the Mind, you are unaware of its most secret and essential ramifications, those fossil imprints so close to our own origins, those tracks we are occasionally able to discover deep in the most unexplored deposits of our minds.

In the name of your own logic we say to you, Life stinks Gentlemen. Look at yourselves for a moment, consider your products. A whole generation of gaunt and bewildered youth is passing through the sieve of your diplomas. You are a plague on the world, Gentlemen, and so much the better for the world, but let it consider itself a little less in the vanguard of humanity.

We need confused adepts, more than active adepts.

ADDRESS TO THE POPE

You are not the confessional, O Pope, it is us, but understand us and let Catholicism understand us.

In the name of Family and Country you urge the sale of souls, the unrestricted grinding of bodies.

We have enough paths to cross between our souls and ourselves and enough distance to cover than to put all your masturbating priests and that heap of rash doctrines which supports all the eunuchs of world liberalism between them and us.

As for your Catholic, Christian God, who, like other gods, conceived all evil:

1. You were too much for him.
2. We don't give a damn about your canons, index, sin, confessional, or clergy; we are thinking of a new war—war on you, Pope, dog.

Here the mind confesses to the mind.

From top to bottom of your Roman masquerade, the thing which triumphs is hatred of the soul's immediate truths, of those flames which burn in the very mind. There is no God, Bible or Gospel, there are no words which check the mind.

We are not of the world, O Pope confined to the world, neither earth nor God speaks through you.

The world is the soul's abyss, warped Pope, Pope foreign to the soul. Let us be immersed in our own bodies, leave our souls within our souls. We don't need your enlightening razor edge.

ADDRESS TO THE DALAI LAMA

We are your most faithful servants, O Grand Lama.

Grant us, grace us with your wisdoms in a language our contaminated European minds can understand. And, if necessary, transform our Minds, make our minds wholly oriented towards those perfect summits where the Human Mind no longer suffers.

Make us a Mind without Habits, a spirit truly frozen in the Mind, or a Mind with the purest habits, your habits, if these are right for freedom.

We are surrounded by roughneck popes, scribblers, critics and dogs. Our Minds have gone to the dogs, whose thoughts are in direct contact with the earth, who think incorrigibly in the present.

Teach us physical levitation of the body, O Lama, and how we may no longer remain earthbound.

For you well know what transparent liberations of the soul we are referring to, what freedom of Mind in the Mind, O acceptable Pope, O true Pope in the Mind.

I behold you with my inner eye, O Pope, on my inward summit. I resemble you, inwardly I, impetus, idea, lip, levitation, dream, cry, renunciation of idea, hovering among all forms and hoping only for the wind.

LETTER TO THE BUDDHIST SCHOOLS

You who are not imprisoned in the flesh, who know at what point in its carnal trajectory, in its senseless comings and goings the soul finds the absolute verb, the new word, the inner land. You know how we turn back into our thoughts, how the mind saves itself from itself. You who are inside yourselves, whose mind is no longer on a physical level, here are hands for which taking is not everything, minds which see further than a forest of roofs, a flowering of façades, a nation on wheels, activity of fire and marble. Whether these iron men advance or words written with the speed of light advance, the sexes advance towards each other with the force of bullets. Yet what will change in the soul's paths, the heart's spasms or the mind's frustrations?

Hurl all these whites into the ocean, therefore, they who arrive with their small brains and well-behaved minds. These curs must understand us. We are not talking about the old human ailment. Our mind suffers from other needs than those inherent in life. We suffer from corruption, the corruption of Reason.

Logical Europe endlessly crushes the mind between the jaws of two extremes, opening and closing the mind. But now this strangulation is at its peak. We must have suffered too long under the yoke. The mind is greater than the mind, life's metamorphoses are manifold. Like you, we reject progress. Come, tear down our houses.

Let our hacks continue to write for a while, our journalists to gossip, our critics to blunder on, our Jews to slip into their pattern of plunder, our politicians to harangue and our judicial assassins to brood over their crimes in peace. *We* know what life is. Our writers, thinkers, doctors, and dunces have agreed to let life down. Let all these hacks slander us, let them slander us from habit or mania, let them slander us from spiritual emasculation, from being unable to attain these lights and shades, these glazed clays, these revolving earths, where man's lofty spirit is always changing. We have captured thought best. Come. Save us from these larvae. Devise new dwellings for us.

LETTER TO THE MEDICAL DIRECTORS OF LUNATIC ASYLUMS

Gentlemen,

Law and Custom allow you the right to evaluate human minds. You are supposed to exercise this sovereign, redoubtable jurisdiction with discernment. You won't mind if we laugh. The credulity of civilised peoples, scholars and administrators, endows psychiatry with limitless supernatural wisdom. Your profession's case is awarded the verdict in advance. We have no intention of discussing the validity of your science here, nor the doubtful existence of mental sickness. But for a hundred pretentious pathogenic diagnoses, in which confusion between mind and matter runs wild, for a hundred classifications only the vaguest of which are still any use, how many noble attempts have been made to approach the world of the mind, in which so many of your prisoners live? For instance, for how many of you are a schizophrenic's dreams and the images which haunt him anything more than a jumble of words?

We are not surprised to find you unequal to a task for which few are preordained. But we vigorously protest against the right attributed to certain men, narrow-minded or not, to sanction their investigations into the domain of the mind with sentences of life imprisonment.

And what imprisonment! We all know—no, it is not widely enough known—that asylums, far from being *asylums*, are fearful jails, where the inmates provide a source of free and useful manpower and where brutality is the rule, all of which you tolerate. A mental asylum, under cover of science and justice, is comparable to a barracks, a prison or a slave colony.

We will not raise the question of arbitrary confinement. This will save you the trouble of making hasty denials. But we categorically state that a great number of your inmates, quite mad by official definition, are also arbitrarily confined. We protest against any interference with the free development of delirium. It is as legitimate, as logical as any other sequence of human ideas or acts. The repression of anti-social reactions is as chimerical as it is unacceptable in principle. All individual acts are anti-social. Madmen, above all, are individual victims of social dictatorship. In the name of individuality which specifically belongs to man, we demand the liberation of these people convicted of sensibility. For we tell you no laws are powerful enough to lock up all men who think and act.

Without stressing the perfectly inspired nature of the manifestations of certain madmen, in so far as we are capable of appreciating them, we simply affirm that their concept of reality is absolutely legitimate, as are all the acts resulting from it.

Try and remember *that* tomorrow morning during your rounds, when, without knowing their language, you attempt to converse with these people over whom, you must admit, you have only one advantage, namely force.

ACTIVITIES OF THE SURREALIST RESEARCH BUREAU[1]

The occurrence of an objective Surrealist revolution is applicable to all states of mind,

to all types of human activity,

to all world conditions within the mind,

to all established moral fact,

to every class of mind.

This revolution aims at a general devaluation, at a depreciation of the mind, at taking the self-evident off the gold standard and at renewed wholesale confusion in language,

at unlevelling thought.

It aims to break up logic and disqualify it. It will then hound it down until it is eradicated from its last primal positions.

It aims to reclassify things spontaneously, in accordance with a deeper and more precise order, inexplicable by means of ordinary reasoning, but an order none the less,

[1] These notes, which idiots will judge from a serious point of view and clever people from a linguistic point of view, are one of the first models, one of the first aspects of what I understand by Confusion in my speech. They are addressed to those whose minds are confused, to those made aphasics by stops in their speech. Yet these notes are the heart of the matter. Here thought is lacking, here the mind shows its members. Yet these are idiotic notes, initial notes, as someone said, "in the articulations of their thought". But subtle notes really.

What well-adjusted mind cannot discern incessant redress of language or tension after deficiency, a knowledge of deviation, accepting the badly expressed. These notes despise language and spit on thought.

Yet between the faults in such humanly ill-constructed, unequally developed thought, shines the will to meaning. The will to bring to light the detours of something badly made as yet, namely the will to believe.

Here a certain Faith comes into it,

but let the coprolitics hear me, the aphasics and in general all those discredited by words and the word, the pariahs of Thought.

I am only speaking to them.

discernible by some sense or other . . . but still discernible, an order which is not completely the property of death.

The break we have made with the world has been clearly established. We do not speak to make ourselves understood. We only speak within ourselves, with ploughshares of anguish, with the cutting edge of fierce obstinacy, we turn thought over, we unlevel it.

The Central Surrealist Research Bureau is to devote itself with all its might to reclassifying life in this way.

An entire philosophy of Surrealism, or something which may be taken as such, must be laid down.

Strictly speaking, this is not a matter of establishing canons and precepts but of finding:

1. Means of carrying out Surrealist investigations into the heart of Surrealist thought.
2. Establish landmarks and means of charting its channels and islands.

Up to a certain point, we can and must concede a Surrealist mystique, a certain order of evasive beliefs with regard to ordinary reasoning, but nevertheless well-defined, relevant to clearly fixed positions in the mind.

Surrealism records certain categories of repulsion rather than beliefs.

Surrealism is above all a state of mind, it does not cry up formulae.

The first point is to try and put oneself in the right frame of mind.

No Surrealist is in the land of the living or thinks of himself in the present, nor does he believe in the effectiveness of the mind as spur, the mind as guillotine, the mind as judge or the mind as doctor, his hopes lie side by side with the mind.

A Surrealist has judged the mind.

He has no feelings which are part of himself and acknowledges no thought whatsoever. His thoughts do not concoct any world to which he can *rationally* subscribe.

He despairs attaining his own mind.

But still, he is in the mind, he judges himself from

within and in the face of his ideas the world does not carry much weight. But in the gap left by some loss, some lapse from himself, some instantaneous reabsorption of the mind, he will see the white creature appear, the vitreous, thinking creature.

This is why he is a Head, he is the sole Head to emerge in the present. In the name of his inner freedom, in the name of his demanding perfection, peace and purity, he spits on you, world, given up as you are to desiccating reason, bogged down in age-old mimicry, having built your houses of words and set up your lists of precepts in which the Surrealist mind can never explode, the only mind worthy of uprooting us.

FURTHER LETTER ABOUT MYSELF

Dear . . .

This is a bad time for me, besides all times are disgusting for me in the state I am in. You have no idea how far I can be deprived of ideas. I do not even have ideas which ought to conform with my body, with my condition as a physical animal, subject to things and gushing out at the multiplicity of their contacts.

We won't discuss the mental animal. The things I admire, the things I have a taste for, are sought by the intellectual animal, but it does not go out of its way to look for them. The living animal. The aggregate of consciousness must not fall apart. What makes me laugh about mankind, about all mankind, is they cannot imagine their conscious aggregate falling apart. Whatever mental process they engage in, they are sure of their aggregate. This aggregate which fills up each of the tiniest chinks in the least suspected mental processes, at whatever stage of evolution or enlightenment these processes come in the mind. It is not that, it is never that. For if we always had to think of our thoughts, we wouldn't be able to think, would we, or to devote ourselves to mental processes higher than thought proper. Not the sweat, secreted by the mind, but this sweat's mechanism. I consider I have pestered people enough with accounts of the distributive quotas in my mind, my awful psychic dearth, and I think they have the right to expect something else from me than cries of incapability and the enumeration of my inability, or I should keep silent. But the problem precisely is, I am alive. Those things which are able to tear men away from their homes, those homes in the mind fenced in by its limits, are outside the field of thought strictly speaking and to me are above relationships in the mind. I am like a blind man in the midst of ideas. I am forbidden any hypotheses which are not affidavits or even simple discussions of known phenomena. But looking at the matter closely, the trouble is I cannot see the innovation, or to speak more correctly, the need for any intellectual process whatsoever. There is no shock to the mind which appears to me to result from an *Idea*, I mean a fostering blaze of powers with new features.

I have reached the point where I no longer feel ideas as ideas, like meetings between mental things, having the magnetism, prestige, the inspiration of total spirituality in them, but as ordinary things combined. I no longer feel them or see them, they are no longer able to rouse me as such and this is probably the reason why I let them pass through my mind without recognising them. My conscious aggregate is broken. I have lost the feeling of the mind, of whatever can properly be thought about, or this whirls about in me like a completely free system, then returns to its chimeras. Before long, perception dims. And something like bits of little thoughts swim about, a *descriptive* light shed on the world. What a world!

But pride has a place in the midst of this nameless misery which also wears an expression of consciousness. This is knowledge through exhaustion, if you like, a sort of low cry which instead of rising, falls. My mind is open through the belly and from below it piles up dark, inexpressible knowledge full of subterranean tides, concave blocks and frozen turbulence. Do not mistake this for imagery. It cries out to take shape as loathsome understanding. I crave only silence from whoever has any regard for me, but if I may venture to say so, intellectual silence, like my waiting, on edge.

Antonin Artaud

INVOCATION TO THE MUMMY

These nares of flesh and bone
Where the shades of the Ultimate
Begin, and the colouring of those lips
You close like a curtain

And this gold life slips you in dreams
Which strips you of bones
And the flowers of that false look
Linking you with light

Mummy, and those spindly hands
To turn your guts over
Those hands whose dreadful shadow
Assumes the shape of a bird

All this in which death decks itself
Like an aleatory rite
The shadows chatter and the gold
In which your black guts are steeped

That way I will join you
Along the roasted, venular way
And your gold like my distress
Is the worst and surest witness.

DIALOGUE IN 1928

Question? Answer. A simple matter, finding equivalents. It implies all the optimism of conversation. The thoughts of the two speakers follow different paths. But any momentary relation between these thoughts, even though contradictory, strikes them as a coincidence. All in all, very comforting, since you enjoy nothing better than asking or replying. The "Exquisite Corpse" produced questions and answers as was intended and the connection between them, so carefully unexpected, was also clearly guaranteed. We have no objection to those who are worried about this thinking they can only see here a more or less perceptible improvement in the rules of the game of *Consequences*.

ANTONIN ARTAUD AND ANDRE BRETON

A. Does Surrealism still hold the same importance in the organisation and disorganisation of our lives?
B. It is all mud, almost entirely composed of flowers.

*

A. How many more times do you think you will fall in love?
B. A soldier stands in a sentry-box. He is alone. He is looking at a snap-shot he has taken out of his wallet.

*

A. Is death of any importance to you in organising your life?
B. It is time to go to bed.

*

A. What is immortal love?
B. Poverty is no sin.

*

A. Night or the maelstrom?
B. Just a shadow.

*

A. What disgusts you most about love?
B. You, my dear friend, and me.

TOXIC KNUCKLE BONES

I evoke the bite of non-existence and imperceptible cohabitation. Here, psychiatrists, I summon you to the bedside of this bloated man who still breathes. Gather about this body stretched out, laying on your gibes, with your bags of loathsome stuffs. It is lost, it is INTOXICATED, I say, your overthrown barriers *have shaken him*, your hollow phantoms, your chirruping, scorched men. *He is shaken.* Therefore trample on this empty body, this transparent body which defied the proscription. It is DEAD. It has been through that hell you promised it, beyond the liquefaction of its bones, and a strange spiritual liberation which was the ultimate danger to you. And now its interlaced nerves keep it in subjection!

Oh, medicine, here is a man who has TOUCHED danger. You have won, psychiatry, you have WON yet he has gone beyond you. The ant's nest of dreams disturbs his limbs in sleep. A concentration of hostile wills relaxes him, raises sorts of sudden obstacles within him. The sky caves in with a great crash. What does he feel? He has lost any feeling of himself. He escaped you through thousands of openings. You think you have hold of him, yet he goes free. He does not belong to you.

He does not belong to you, DENOMINATION. What is your evil sensibility aimed at? To return him to his mother's care, to make him the waste pipe, the drain for the very smallest mental confraternity, for the very smallest conscious common denominator.

Rest easy. HE IS CONSCIOUS.

But he is the greatest Great Consciousness.

But he is the base of a breath which bows your head with serious madness, for at least he has won that. He has overthrown Insanity. And now, legibly, consciously, clearly, universally, it blows on your palace of petty madness, it points a finger at you, frightened, little and shivering, retreating before All-life.

For floating on grandiloquent members, on thick flipper hands, hearts enlightened in tempo with fear, perceiving the infinity of an insect growling on the floor, glimpsing the thousand and one itches of nightly solitude, the forgiveness for being abandoned, knocking its head against endless brick walls, head agape, breaking into tears to lay a useless and clearly warped penis out on a shaky table,

finally to *spirt out*, to *spirt out* with the most formidable head in the face of a thousand, sudden breaks in an unstable existence, to void life on the one side and the return to the void of crystalline freedom on the other,

thus at the basis of this poisoning verbalism there lies the floating paroxysm of a free body returning to its origins, the wall of death being transparent, cut down, thrown down. For death behaves in this way, by a thread of anguish the body cannot avoid going through. The boiling wall of anguish first provokes terrible contractions, aboriginal, organic release such as a disconsolate child might dream about. At this parental meetingplace, dreamy memories emerge—forgotten ancestral faces. A whole rendezvous of human races to which so-and-so belongs. The first enlightenment of toxic fury.

This is the strange light of narcotics which crushes ominously familiar space.

In the throbbing of the solitary night, that ant-like noise occurs which discoveries, revelations, and apparitions make, these great abortive bodies taking wind and wing again, the immense quivering of Survival. The drug arrives with its sane face at this convention of corpses. Timeless arrangements begin. Death at first wears an expression of Regret. Sovereign desolation sets the tone for so many dreams which only ask to be awakened. What do you say? Would you deny the repercussions of those kingdoms which are only the beginning for me!

IN THE DARK OR THE SURREALIST BLUFF

For some time now, the issue between Surrealists and

me has no longer been whether they drove me out or whether I walked out on their grotesque sham.[1] I left because I had had enough of that dragged-out masquerade. Besides, I was quite certain the Surrealists would do no more within the new framework they had chosen, than in any other. Time and events have not failed to prove me right.

One wonders what difference it would make to the world if the Surrealists came to terms with the Revolution or if the Revolution took place over and above the Surrealist venture, considering how little the Surrealists have been able to influence the manners and ideas of the times.

Besides, is there still a Surrealist venture or didn't Surrealism die the day Breton and his adepts thought they ought to join with Communism and look to the field of events and contiguous matter for the outcome of acts which normally could only develop within the inmost compass of the brain.

They thought themselves free to jeer at me when I spoke of a metamorphosis of inner states of the soul.[2] As if I

[1] *I need hardly stress the fact that the Surrealists* could find nothing better to pull me to pieces than to use my own written work. I would like to make it clear that the note appearing at the bottom of pages 6 & 7 of the pamphlet "In the Open", aimed at blasting the very basis of my actions, is a pure and simple reproduction, a thinly disguised copy extracts taken from pieces aimed at them. In these, I undertook to set out their actions in their true colours, all choked as they are with wretched hatred and short-lived impulses. I got together the material for an article out of these bits and pieces, two or three magazines rejecting it in turn, among them the *N.R.F.*, as being too compromising. It makes little difference what informer helped to get the article into their hands. The important thing is they found it embarrassing enough to feel the need to counteract its effect. As to accusations I meant for them, which they later turned against me, I would rather not leave it to their foul methods, but to those who know me well, to decide between us.

The whole basis, all the exacerbation of our quarrel revolves around the word "Revolution".

[2] As if a man who had experienced the limitations of his acts once and for all and who refused to commit himself beyond what he consciously believed those limitations to be, were less noteworthy from a revolutionary point of view than some make-believe bawler who, in the stifling world we live in, an eternally motionless, closed world, invokes some insurrectional state or other to judge actions and gestures everyone well knows he will not do.

This is very precisely what made me sick of Surrealism. Reflecting on the inborn incapability, the congenital weakness of these Gentlemen, as against their perpetually ostentatious attitude, their threats into the air, their understood soul to mean the same disgusting thing they do. And as if, from an Ultimate point of view, seeing the world's social structure change and power pass from the hands of the bourgeoisie into those of the proletariat could ever be of the slightest interest.

If this was what the Surrealists were really after, at

blasphemings into the void. And what are they doing now but once more displaying their incapability, their insuperable sterility? Because I refused to commit myself beyond my self, because I called for silence about me, faithful in thought and actions to what I felt to be my deep, irremissible incapability, these Gentlemen considered my presence inconvenienced them. But what appeared most reprehensible and blasphemous to them was that I wanted the fixing of my limitations to be left up to me, that I insisted on remaining free and master of my own actions. For what does the entire world Revolution mean to me when I know I am to remain in endless pain and misery in the depths of my own charnel-house. No man should ever want to consider anything beyond his own deep sensitivity, his inmost ego. This is a completely Revolutionary standpoint to me. The only revolution that is any good is one I benefit from. Me and people like me. The revolutionary strength of any movement is its ability to upset the present basis of things, to offset the angle of reality.

But in a letter written to the Communists they admit their complete lack of preparation in the field in which they have just enlisted. More than that, the type of action asked of them is incompatible with their true spirit.

Whatever spirit they may have, this is where we are in agreement, at least partly, in inhibitions of a similar nature, although due to far more serious, far more significant reasons for me than for them. In the end they own themselves unable to do what I have always refused to attempt. As to Surrealist action itself, I have no qualms. They can do little else but prepare it. Recording, re-recording the exact state of their inner lives, like any old Stendhal, these Amiels of the Communist Revolution. The idea of a Revolution will never be anything but an idea to them, without this idea, in ageing, taking on the ghost of any effectiveness.

But don't they see they are revealing the futility of the Surrealist movement itself, Surrealism unsullied by any contamination, when they feel a need to break off its inner growth, its true development, buttressing it up by adhering in principle or fact to the French Communist Party. Was this the rebellious movement, that fire at the basis of the whole of reality? In order to stay alive did Surrealism need to embody itself in a factual rebellion, to merge with such and such demands concerning an eight-hour day, or salary negotiations, or the struggle against the high cost of living. What a joke and what baseness in their souls. Yet this is surely what they seem to be saying, that joining the French Communist Party appeared the logical consequence of the development of Surrealist ideas and its sole ideological safeguard!!!

But I deny that the logical development of Surrealism should have led it to the clearly defined form of revolution that goes under the name of Marxism. I always thought a movement as independent as Surrealism was not subject to the processes of normal logic. Besides, this contradiction is not likely to bother the Surrealists very much, readily disposed as they are to let nothing slip by which might be to their advantage, or anything that might be of temporary use to them. Mention Logic, they will answer illogic, but mention Illogic, Chaos, Incoherence or Freedom and they will answer Necessity, Law, Duty and Exactitude. Their machinations are founded on such fundamental bad faith.

least you could excuse them. Their aims would be trite and restricted but at least they would exist. But they do have the most limited goal towards which they can initiate action and when have they ever given a damn about formulating one?

Besides, can one work towards a goal? Are motives enough? Do the Surrealists think they can justify their expectations by the simple fact of being conscious they have them? Expectancy is not a state of mind. If you don't do anything you don't run the risk of falling flat on your face. Yet this is not reason enough to get talked about.

I despise life too much to think any sort of change which might develop in the structure of appearances could change anything in my hateful condition. The thing that sets me apart from the Surrealists is that they are as fond of life as I despise it. Revelling in every opportunity through every pore is the centre point of their obsessions. But is not asceticism an integral part of true magic, even the most disgusting, even the blackest. The devilish reveller himself has an ascetic side, a certain spirit of mortification.

I am not referring to their written works which are resplendent, although ineffectual in the way they consider them. I am referring to their principal attitude, the pattern of their entire lives. I do not hate any of them individually. I condemn and reject them as a whole, rendering to each one of them all the esteem and even all the admiration they deserve for their work and their minds. In any case from that point of view I would not be as childish as they are to suddenly turn on them and deny them any talent the moment they stopped being my friends. Luckily this is not the case.

The case in point was displacing the world's mental axis, unlevelling appearances, and transfiguring feasibility. Surrealism was to contribute to bring these about. All matter begins with spiritual disturbance. To leave it up to objects and their transformation to guide us is brutishly obscene, a profiteer in reality's viewpoint. No one has ever understood and the Surrealists themselves do not understand and cannot foresee where their Revolutionary will is to lead them. Unable to conceive or imagine a Revolution which would not evolve within a heart-breakingly materialistic framework, they leave it to fate, to a certain accidental deficiency and incapability peculiar to them, to explain their inertia and eternal sterility.

Surrealism was never anything else than a new sort of magic to me. Imagination and dreams, all this intensive freeing of the unconscious whose aim was that those things the soul is accustomed to hiding should break through, and must of necessity usher in a profound transformation in the scale of appearances, in the value of meanings and creative symbolism. Concrete matter entirely changes its garb, its shell and no longer applies to the same mental gestures. The beyond, the unseen, reject reality. The world collapses.

Then we can start examining our illusions and stop pretending.

Let the occult's thick walls crumble down once and for all on these incapable gabblers, on these revolutionaries who revolutionise nothing and who waste their lives in rebukes and empty threats.

These brutes urge me to become converted. I certainly am in great need of it. But at least I admit I am weak and sullied. I aspire to another life. And, all in all, I would rather be in my shoes than in theirs.[1]

What is left of the Surrealist venture? Very little except

[1] This bestiality I am referring to, which disgusts them so much, is however what distinguishes them best. Their love of direct pleasure, that is to say materialism, has made them lose their original direction, that splendid power of escape whose secret we thought they were going to dispense. A spirit of disorder and petty cavilling drives them to tear one another apart. Yesterday it was Soupault and I who left sickened by the whole business. Before that it was Roger Vitrac, whose expulsion was one of their first dirty tricks.

They may well howl in their corner and say it is not so. My answer is that for me Surrealism was always an insidious extension of the unseen, the unconscious near at hand. Riches of the unseen unconscious become tangible, controlling speech directly it comes into one's head.

For me Ruysbroeck, Martinez de Pasqualis and Boehme are sufficient justification. Any mental act, if it is sound, materialises at the right moment. The inner states of the soul! But they bear with them their rock-hard, real action garb. This is an established fact, established by itself, irremissibly implied.

high hopes deceived. But in the field of literature itself, they may in fact have brought something new. This anger, this scalding disgust poured down on things in writing, forms a fruitful attitude which may be useful one day, later on. Literature has been purified by this and brought closer to the mind's essential truths. But that is all. There are no positive gains beyond literature or imagery, yet that was the only fact that mattered. From a correct use of dreams might be born a new way of regulating one's thoughts, of behaving among appearances. Psychological truth stripped of all parasitic, useless appendages and more closely held. We were alive then, sure enough, but it may be a law of the mind that forsaking reality can never lead to anything but illusion. Within the scanty limits of our tangible field, we are pressured, beguiled on all sides. This was clearly shown in the abberation which led revolutionaries at the highest possible level literally to abandon that level, to attach its practical, utilitarian meaning to the word Revolution, the social meaning asserted to be the sole valid one, since one doesn't want to be taken in by words. Strange reflection on one's conduct, strange levelling.

Can anyone think that to advance a simple moral attitude is enough, if this attitude is wholly characterised by inertia? Surrealism's inner nature leads it as far as Revolution. This is a positive fact. It is the only possible effective conclusion (so they say). Yet a large number of Surrealists refused to adopt it. But what about the others, what did throwing their lot in with Communism bring them, what did they have to give up? They made no progress by it. Within the enclosed circle of my self, I never felt the need for this development ethic of whatever would apparently enhance the Revolution. I place the logical requirements of my own reality above all real needs. This seems the only valid logic to me, not some higher logic whose irradiations only affect me in so far as they come into contact with my sensibility. There are no disciplines I feel obliged to submit to, however close the reasoning may be to inveigle me to adopt them.

Two or three principles of life and death stand above any risky submissiveness for me. And any logic whatsoever has always seemed only borrowed to me.

*

Surrealism died because of the idiotic sectarianism o its adepts. What is left is a sort of hybrid mass the Surrealsists themselves are incapable of naming. Perpetually on the borders of appearances, unsuited to take root in life, Surrealism is still seeking a solution, marking time in its own tracks. Incapable of choosing, of making up its mind wholly for lies or wholly for the truth (true lies of mental deception, false truth of reality at hand, but destructible). Surrealism is always hunting for this unfathomable, indefinable rift in reality where it can apply its formerly powerful leverage, now fallen into the hands of eunuchs. But my mental deficiency, my well-known cowardice, refuses to find the least interest in upheavals that would only affect this external, directly perceptible side of reality. An external metamorphosis, in my opinion, can only be something supplementary. The social level, the materialistic level towards which the Surrealists are steering their poor vague yearnings for action, their forever potential hatreds, is to me only a useless, implied show.

I know all free men are on my side in this dispute, all the true revolutionaries who think personal freedom is a higher good than anything conquered, or any gains made on a relative level.

*

My scruples when confronted with all real action?

These scruples are unconditional and are of two kinds. They are ultimately aimed at the ingrained sense of deep uselessness of any spontaneous or unspontaneous act.

This is a completely pessimistic stand. But a certain type of pessimism conveys its own clear-sightedness. The lucidity of despair, the senses irritated as if on the edge of the abyss. And side by side with the awful relativity of any human acts, this unconscious spontaneousness urging us to act despite everything.

Also in the ambiguous, unfathomable realm of the unconscious; warnings, perspectives, glimpses of an entire life which grows as one looks at it, revealing itself still able to disturb the mind.

These are the scruples we hold in common. But with the Surrealists, it seems they were settled in favour of action. Once they admitted the necessity for such action, they lost no time in declaring themselves unable to carry it out. This is a field from which they were alienated forever by the configuration of their minds.

As to what concerns me, have I ever said anything else? All the same, there are desperately abnormal psychological and physiological circumstances in my favour, of which they would not know how to avail themselves.

SEVEN LETTERS

TO MADAME TOULOUSE

Marseilles, July 1921

My mind is very disturbed these days but it would not add anything to tell you why or give you details. I did not buy any more of the *Cahiers d'Aujourd'hui* after No. 2 as it was useless to load myself up with them for the trip. However, if you could get me the back numbers of *Crapouillot* from 1 June it would be a way of passing the time pleasantly during the vacation and also Chesterton's novel entitled *A Man Called Thursday* published by the *N.R. Française*. Also perhaps Conrad's *Typhoon* by the same publishers. There is nothing like this here. I do not feel like reading anything else but adventure stories which does not mean they are devoid of intellectuality. They contain more than others, but it is intellectuality in action.

No, familiarity with Rimbaud does not show in what I am doing; this stems, however, from my having the same preoccupations. Contrary to what one might think, I have read Rimbaud only once and for such poems, especially for those in prose, there is nothing to them. How different from Edgar Allen Poe. One could say he really influenced me. Besides, we should wait until I have really expressed myself. Up to now I have only done one or two poems which show what I could become. Besides, one must be in possession of one's mind in its *entirety*, something I have never achieved.

I will be at Evian about 3 August.

Antonin Artaud

TO DR. ALLENDY

Paris, 30 November 1927

My Dear Friend,

Did I tell you that the psychoanalysis sessions I finally consented to made an unforgettable impression on me. You well knew when I met you how I showed a specially instinctive nervous repulsion for this type of treatment. You succeeded in changing my mind, perhaps not from an intellectual point of view, for in this inquisitiveness, in this probing into my conscious by an alien intellect there is a sort of "prostitution", a shamelessness I will always reject, but from an experimental point of view I was able to note the benefit I derived from it. And if need be, I will consent to a similar attempt but from the depths of my soul I am determined to avoid psychoanalysis, I will always avoid it as I will always avoid all attempts to hem my consciousness in with concepts or formulae, with any verbal systematisation. For all that, I will testify to the change your achievement has brought about in me. However, and this is the reason I am writing to you, there is a tendency among those around me, which you especially share, to believe me *cured*, to think I have returned to normal life and for my case to have ceased to be medically justifiable. This is not so. I still have a great need, I essentially need help from someone like you, provided you will agree to amend your opinion about me. I can very well see the tendency people have to believe I have picked up and am in a glowing phase of my existence, that the fates are good to me, shower me with gifts, with blessings. In fact on the surface everything seems to substantiate it, I seem to be blessed by the gods as much materially as morally and mentally. Well, there is something decayed in me, there is a sort of fundamental flaw in my psychism which prevents me enjoying what fate has to offer. I am telling you this so you will still believe I need your help and will not drop all further interest in me. I am completely sane, sharper than ever, what I am lacking is an object on which to focus, an inner substance. This is more serious and distressing than you think. I would like to go beyond this blank, futile spot. This marking time cripples me, and makes me inferior to everyone and everything. I am lifeless, I am lifeless!!! My inner enthusiasm is dead. It is years since I recovered it, years since I felt the spark which saves me. This spontaneity in ideas, harbinger of one's ego, where my personality rediscovers itself, surveys itself, discovers its density, its precious resonance. Nothing but listlessness fills my mind. Everything I light on, impressions and ideas, I discover them it seems, as if by chance, they are memories stuck together, with only the appearance of a new life—and their quality is *affected*. This is not just imagination, or just an impression. The fact is, I am no longer myself, my true ego is asleep. I am moving towards my imagery. I gather it in slow handfuls, it does not come to me or assert itself in me. Under such conditions, I have no criteria. This imagery, whose truth gives it its value, is now worthless, being only figurative, a reflection of thoughts previously mulled over, or mulled over by others, not actually personally *thought*. Understand me, this is not a question of the quality of the impressions or the quantity of ideas, rather the electrifying *vivacity* of truth and reality. Life no longer exists, life does not inspire or accompany the things I think. I say LIFE. I did not say the colourings of life. I mean real life, the essential inspiration. Being, the initial spark where all thoughts catch fire—this nucleus. I feel the nucleus inside me is dead. I am suffering, I suffer at each of my mental emanations. I suffer from their absence, from the virtuality all my thought *inevitably* passes through and in which MY THOUGHT is absorbed and turns in circles. Always the same trouble. I cannot succeed in *thinking*. Do you understand this hollowness, this enduring intense void. This vegetating. How horribly I am vegetating. I can neither advance nor return. I am held, always localised around the same spot all my books express. Only now, I have left my books behind me. I cannot transcend them, for in order to transcend them first of all one would have to *live*. And I persist in not living. I am trying to make you understand how. This is because my thoughts no longer extend either in time or space. I am nothing, I have no ego. For when confronted by whatever conjecture or circumstance may arise, I do not think anything. My thoughts do not suggest anything. I search in vain. I have nothing, either from an intellectual aspect or from an emotional or purely imaginary aspect. I have nothing in reserve. Without any kind of possibility.

I have no reason to look for ideas. I KNOW I will never discover my ideas. Nothing will ever arise within me to attain the degree of mental strength, the inner compression where my ego could appear or find itself. As long as I cannot rediscover my personal fulguration, a visionary intensity, *a range* of ideas born with ease, I mean born and not induced or fabricated, all my work will be unreliable, for it will be born under false conditions, and such that all men but me do not know it. Everything I write is not created, does not share in creation, has the appearance of a make-shift, not made up here a little and there a little, but unnecessarily and for lack of something else. I swear, my dear friend, this is serious, very serious. I am vegetating in the worst moral sloth. I never work. What comes out of me seems drawn by chance. And I could write or say or think completely differently from what I say or think and it would be just as representative of me. That is to say, just as badly. That is to say, not at all. I am not here. I am not, will never more be here. This is serious because it is not a matter of gratuitous written work or imagery to fit the imagery, it is a matter of total thought, that is to say, life. The same vacuity takes hold of me about any circumstances in life. Still the business of the letters to Rivière. I know I annoy everyone and interest no one, but what am I to do since I am alive? Unless I *die*, there is no escape. Were I to die, or were you to understand me, knowing *how little* my life, which deludes so many people, *is worth* at present, could you find a medical means to get me out of this?

Yours. Your friend.

Artaud

P.S. Thanks for the pills but I devoured the last of them a fortnight ago. Meanwhile I will need 3 weeks' supply at Cannes. I would need at least forty strong ones, for as you will guess I have fallen back into the habit. Alas!!!

TO MADAME YVONNE ALLENDY

Nice, 24 February 1929

My Dear Friend,

I do not remember you ever mentioning the Paris–

Saigon or Paris–Hanoi service. I thought I had made it up myself. This is why the coincidence surprised me. But I would not have been so moved, if I had not been without news from you for so long. In any case, your letter has completely reassured me.

As to the other matter, it goes without saying I would never have dreamed of using these same scenarios. But fate has done a good job so we must think, for I have severe pains in my head and I am incapable of undertaking any interesting work whatsoever. This is so, whatever all the doctors on earth may say or think. I am afflicted. *There is no end to it.* I am also writing to the doctor to try and explain myself, but I need his practical help. With the passing of time, I can clearly see my condition is not dependent on drugs. Otherwise it would be too easy to explain. I used to be intimately understood. I must be freed, once and for all, or else I am finished. I assure you I am not exaggerating. At present my life is one long torture. I know what I am exposed to. Please believe how awful it is, despite appearances. If it were only a question of restricted activity, in fact it would not be a big thing, but there is the suffering besides. This big, swollen head, nerves continually flayed bare, this jammed vitality, limbs hard to move, full of discomfort and internal, *physical* obstacles. You cannot imagine what agony it can be. And the worst of it is that since I am not able to achieve a single externalised state, people are tempted not to believe me or to think I am unduly exaggerating. I assure you I can be excused for panicking so easily. For a long time now I have had no ordinary standards to measure by.

As to my book, I am not very surprised:

1. Not to have heard from my publisher.
2. To find out he is probably waiting to bring out Vitrac's book as well in order to bring mine out.

Is my old persecution complex aroused again or isn't there any scheming or at least pressure, some insistence or other on Vitrac's part, who is right there putting his case to Denoël, perhaps to the detriment of mine? Couldn't you let me know what you can find out?

Another thing. I received a copy of a circular letter addressed to all the Surrealists by one of their members. You can imagine what I would reply if need be. The scurrilous blindness of these old relics is unparalleled. Their sense of opportunism, too!!! All this is not worth the tediousness of an answer, but I would be interested to find out if this is an individual effort, or if all the cronies agreed to it. Try to get hold of a copy and read it. I have definitely taken my stand. My future is settled from that angle. They are just as I had profoundly judged them. Without any psychology or breadth of mind. No sense either of mankind or Life, nor of the state of the times, That goes for *all of them*, even the best. The same terrible irreparable, lacunae which definitely rendered them incapable of remaining aloof for a moment, full of phobias, routine, hateful prejudices, long-simmering hates, without any real magnanimity or greatness. It is a shame the fates keep me in a state of constant and obvious inferiority to myself because they want to and surely *on purpose*. This stops me from revealing the truths I would otherwise have revealed. All those people have had their chance and it is too unfair. And I cannot even count on a revenge in time.

Please accept my sincerest friendship.

Antonin Artaud

TO M. AND MME. ALLENDY

Nice, 22 March, 1929

I have just received the parcel of books but I doubt if I will be able to do anything with them for some time. Things are going from bad to worse, and worse from day to day, to such an extent that I keep asking myself every second whether I won't soon have to drop everything and go and have myself locked away somewhere. The pains I endure are beginning to beggar description. No peace and an agonizing strangle-hold. Shooting pains in the right side of the nape of my neck *which make me gasp for air when they occur*. My limbs grow numb, and full of pins and needles, if ever I hold them still. Violent spasms shifting from my arms to my legs from one minute to the next. My spinal column full of cracks and painful higher up. Ready to drop with brutal exhaustion and an increase *in the unbearable constriction in my head and shoulder blades.* Then at times, a general ache which comes and goes, at other times all the sensations of an intense fever: aches, great heat, shivers, buzzing in my ears, dizziness. This paroxysm drags on day after day. I stopped taking any drugs weeks ago now. What was the use? Then over-excitement and depression follow one another quick as lightning and I am so irritable as to see red, to feel murderous at a tone of voice or a gesture my imagination interprets wrongly.

Horribly tired by the slightest reading. And this weight on my chest. My heart pounding. I will leave it up to you to show the doctor this letter when it will annoy him least. But I swear I am growing terribly worried.

Kindest regards,

A. Artaud

TO MADAME YVONNE ALLENDY

Nice, 3 April 1929

My Dear Friend,

I hope you received my last letter in which I asked you to take the necessary steps to obtain the adaptation rights to the *Master of Ballantrae.* I am suffering from a period when I am marking time again, after five or six days improvement. True, on a doctor's advice I was mistaken enough to follow, I changed the type of shots I was taking at the end of three days for similar shots containing something slightly different. Really, what I am enduring is monstrous. If this goes on for a little while longer I will give in, I will go under. I will die like a dog with my life a failure behind me. One cannot imagine the frightful torment I put up with *at every single moment.* The violence or strength of the pain is nothing, but its deep, total nature attacks being in all its senses, sucking life out with a feeling of *physical exhaustion* at the ego-centre, which absorbs, digests, cuts off or deforms sensibility. Personality has become a sort of magnetism but unbroken and off centre, emitting lines of force at random. It is awful. Yet I look healthy. People compliment me on how well I look yet ask themselves what grief is preying on me. Whereas I am not grieved, there is just the weight of my physico-mental oppression which crushes and stupefies my facial muscles because my head is caught in God knows what trap which does not release its quarry much.

Regards,

A. Artaud

TO M. SOULIÉ DE MORANT

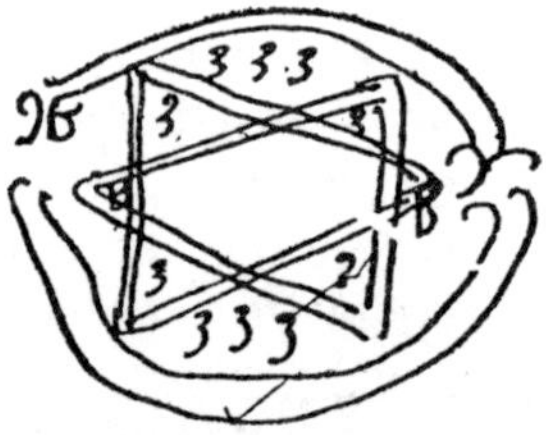

17 February 1932
Thursday Morning.

Dear Sir,

I was surprised and amazed at the way you *divined* my condition, accurately spotting with tremendous precision the deep, disabling, demoralising disorder I have suffered from so long and at the same time I envied how you synthesised it, when presenting it in its true guise, having *felt* it just as it is in its proper place, a faculty of which I am notably deprived.

If I am writing to you it is only because I am concerned at having *none the less* overlooked a characteristic fact which will enable you to look even more deeply and more clearly into my abominable condition. An abominably cruel condition which in truth I have no words to define because I cannot see anything or clearly expose anything in me, precisely because of the doubt affecting me, and whatever my condition:

1. My inner perception and observation.
2. The effectiveness of the means granted to me to em-

brace and show them.

If the mind is attacked, this is so in all cases, of course, and on all levels.

Besides, nothing is more detestable and painful, nothing is more agonizing for me than the doubts expressed on the reality and the nature of the phenomena I am defining.

Sometimes, I am regarded as being too clever in expressing my deficiencies, my deep failings and the incapability I define, for anyone to think they are not imaginary and wholly invented.

They do not doubt the reality of my subjective disorders and the painful state in which I am submerged, but they doubt its objectivity and especially its *scope*.

Now I can never insist on this enough, my condition undergoes infinite variations which go from bad to relatively better. In such improved conditions I become able to think, *feel* and write a little and among other things well enough to believe I would not have saddled myself with a letter like this if I was not somewhat *recovered*. In general people do not realise that if I am speaking and describing my sickness, this is because it has partly disappeared.

All this is elementary and I am of course not saying it for your benefit, but in general I must tirelessly insist on it.

As I told you, I was much sicker than I am at present, a prey to maddening oppression and quartering of my conscious, really *astray* concerning my most elementary perception, unable to collect any ideas, to accumulate anything within me and even less to express anything since I was unable to retain anything.

This was a psychic breakdown just as in the physiological field it is a calamity when the stomach or bowels can no longer retain anything. And physically I found myself under the blows of wild oppression, drawn between the feelings of a complete nervous vacuum, and magnetic repressiveness, equally extreme sweltering heaviness.

Between this dual, manifold sensation, my mind which could not apply itself to anything, also saw itself stripped of the continuity of its inner life, so much so that the impressions born the instant the subconscious links them and is automatically about to shape them, these impressions, these representations, these forms also *took pleasure in provoking* my mind by reabsorbing themselves, breaking apart prematurely and maddening thought which wished to grasp them.

The *line* my condition has taken is the same at present and differs only in degree and intensity. With this additional fact that when these pains, these strange phenomena began, I thought myself completely scuttled. Nevertheless I was able to realise I was sometimes able to do something but now the torment is worst when I am not able to express myself.

Thus always this same state of being oppressed and compressed recurred with less intensity (may the gods make certain sweltering states I know too well never return) and moreover augmented by a feeling of physical remoteness from myself as if I were never going to control my limbs again, or my reflexes, or my most spontaneous mechanical reactions. To this was added a further feeling, rigidity and horrible physical fatigue in my tongue when I spoke, *the strain of thinking* always physically resounding in all my muscles and the stammering I suffer from has varying degrees, but it sometimes disappears altogether and tires me out tremendously (since my earliest childhood—6 to 8 years old—I noticed these periods of stammering and horrible physical contraction of the facial nerves and tongue succeeded periods of calm and perfect ease). All this therefore became complicated by corresponding psychic trouble, but which only appeared *explosively* around the age of 19.

There is a sort of vacuum in the facial muscles which I might be so bold as to call an active vacuum. It manifests itself physically by a sort of dizzy mesmerism of the features. This is not a metaphor and should be taken almost literally. For this physical vertigo was horribly agonizing and the feeling I am describing reached its climax two or three years after the disorder began. At times this feeling was superseded by a sort of moral spasm, virulent agony which bowled me over like a wave of derangement, wherever I happened to be and made me want, not to cry, but to shake with sobs, to howl with despair. Fortunately none of this has come back for a long time and now only a certain number of shifting or localised physical pains are left, a deep overclouding of my conscious which periodically overcomes me, robbing me of my inner representations and my ideas, depriving me of the benefit of the intellectual system I created for myself.

Now I especially suffer:

1. Intellectually on the one hand.
2. Sentimentally and emotionally on the other.

1. The mind's automatism and its continuity having been destroyed, I can only think disjointedly. When I am thinking, the greater part of the stock of terms and the vocabulary I established for my own use is unusable, rusty and *derelict* somewhere, but if the term appears, deepseated thought yields, contact is brutally cut off, the deep nervous emotions no longer respond to thought, automatism is thrown into confusion *and this is at times when I am thinking!!!* When I am not thinking, it is no use calling on my special vocabulary. Now whether someone asks me, or whether I ascertain my own emptiness and endeavour to engender thought, the tragedy starts, this intellectual tragedy in which I am always vanquished.

For it seems impossible to me to have nothing to say, in addition I know that in this sense or that, I formerly had my own way of thinking and concepts have confusedly appeared but woe betide me if I try to elucidate them, to actualise anything. It seems to me I have even forgotten *how to think*. Yes, it is the idea of this particular intellectual vacuum I wanted to *make clear* once and for all. It seems to me the distinguishing characteristic of my condition. This is something no one else can pride themselves on sharing with me, to possess at the same time as me, that is, *forgetting* the forms of thought. This is what is characteristic. And through the forms of thought, also forgetting oneself, the forms of intellectual or moral sensibility, sensibility when confronted with ideas. In such conditions, it is nothing less than a case of forgetting the intellectual content of the mind, of having broken off contact with all the evidence which is the basis of thought.

2. And the sentimental or emotional disorder I mentioned a while ago is closely bound up with this loss and this higher catastrophe, for it is quite clear that the destructive element which depolarises the mind and robs it of its evidence, is not concerned with finding out if the mind will keep its trouble to itself or will apply it to something more impersonal which under other circumstances could have served to compose some work or other, *a production!* After all, we will never know what makes the mind decide to create. The same thoughts, the same willed inclination could after all go towards inflating the ego, to feed it more narrowly, to increase its inner density and too bad for works and creativity, since psychically, the result is the same. But as for myself, this black-out, this weeding out of the higher parts of the conscious and thought are unfortunately valid for all circumstances in life, and if my brain has become intellectually inoperative, it is no more use at times when this vacuum takes over and fills me with anguish and anxiety, makes me feel life is lost and useless. They also have a sentimental value, they manifest themselves in the soul by a colouring of the void, by wholly black emotionalism really fashioned in the image of me, but on the other hand this emotionalism is its lack of resonance, its coagulation. . . .

TO M. SOULIÉ DE MORANT

Nunc salmavat

Friday evening, 19 February 1932

Dear Doctor,

One thing has just about disappeared from my field of attention and no longer forms a part of the characteristics of my condition. This impression of unbelievable fatigue and complete exhaustion, exhaustion which seems to probe the stamina and the whole of man's driving force at all levels and in all senses. With this awful, colossal weariness, this vast unparalleled oppressiveness in the top of the head and the nape of the neck, oppressiveness of such force and it seems a mass of such size, it gives the impression of the weight of the world on one's shoulders. It concentrates some cosmic emotionality or other, reuniting our tactile sensibility, the far-flung contacts with communication between one star and another. The proof is that resting, stretched out on the bed, this feeling, far from disappearing, grows aggravated, transformed into the impression of a painful vacuum of magnetic stress, exerted on the limbs and along the spinal column and encircling the pelvis. During such states, unconscious images still continue, they are not sick but it seems the disorder manifests itself the moment impressions become conscious, however little, become clothed in sensibility, emotion and will-power. As soon as my intellectual willpower steps in, however little, with the aim of allowing an image or an idea to become embodied by taking shape, as soon as I try to enunciate clearly and sanely one of these inner words the mind unendingly associates, the disorder makes its presence and continuity known. It seems sufficient for the mind to have wanted to use an idea or mental picture, for this use to be taken from it and the image enunciated invariably miscarries. To try and bring this idea or impression out is even more difficult and only ends up revealing quicker and in a more glaring manner, the lack of continuity and nervous density underlying my present personality.

The fluctuations in my condition are generally marked by the greater or lesser number of times I complain of a thought which first miscarried in this way!—and then by the level of stratification and evolution or development of this thought at the point where the fault occurs.

That is to say:

accepted all ideas or imagery arise in the unconscious and through the intervention of willpower make up the inner word, the problem is to discover at what point in its formation the fissure will occur, and whether the intervention or manifestation of the will is without doubt one cause of the trouble and occasions the fissure and whether the fissure will interrupt this thought or the next.

In order that it only interrupts the next, the thought or the phrase expressing it must be devilishly short for I am in no condition to dwell, however slightly, on any thought.

The lack of continuity, the lack of range, the lack of endurance of my thought is therefore one of the fundamental characteristics of my condition. Now this lack of endurance which appeared about such and such a minor manifestation of consciousness in more or less tame, uninteresting thoughts, is clearly what prevents me from becoming validly, lastingly conscious of what I am and what I think and the judgements I might infer from them in any way whatsoever. This also prevents me from keeping present in my mind a certain amount of standard images corresponding to my feelings and the personal portrayals in my mind and consequently become and remain conscious of *me*—My vitality and latent lucidity are aroused about a personal, silent, motionless association where I am alone, about a sense outside or about a question asked by others, conversations I overhear, a discussion I am taking part in, I know I will never get very far and that the fissure, the stop, cannot help occurring. It occurs according to the day, mood and length of time when I find my thoughts more or less quickly, permitting me to say more or less what I like, are inevitable and terribly *abnormal*. By this I mean that it is worth asserting that this is patently unhealthy, for the objection has often been raised that these breaks in thought, these obstacles to intellectual revelation, as the saying so well goes, happen to everyone. Yes, but first, infinitely less of them and second, there is also a difference in type and degree: the stop does not affect consciousness and its manifestations to the same degree. Then, if you like, it is one of the threads in the cloth which snaps whereas with me it is the whole bolt, this break momentarily destroys all consciousness, the brain's automatism recoups its losses in other people but does not recover them in me since its very *mechanism* is impaired and its functioning stopped. There is one more comment to be made on this subject. In a way, we might consider the impossibility of formulating and prolonging thought on the same level as the stammering which overcomes my external utterances just about every time I want to speak. Then it is as if my thought shrinks every time it wants to manifest itself and this is the contradiction which slaps my inner thought down inwardly, compresses it like a spasm. The thought, the expression stops because the flow is too powerful, the brain wants to say too many things it thinks all at once, ten thoughts instead of one rush towards the exit, the brain sees thought as a unit, in full detail, and it also sees all the multiple points of view with which it could ally itself and the forms with which it could endow them, a vast, conceptual juxtaposition all seemingly more essential and also more dubious than the next and which all the syntactic brackets in the world would never be enough to express and explain. But to analyse such a state of mind correctly, the conscious does not err because it is brimming over but because it is empty, for this teeming and above all unstable and changeable juxtaposition is an illusion. There was no juxtaposition initially, for it seems clear that in every conscious state there is always a dominant note and if the mind has not chosen a dominant note *mechanically* it is through weakness and because nothing dominated it at that moment, nothing cropped up strongly enough or prolonged enough in the field of consciousness to register. Thus instead of being overloaded with a surplus, there is a shortage instead, without any precise thought being able to find a fissure when it manifests itself and so we have this slackening, disorder and instability.

Incidentally this slackening, disorder and instability are expressed in an endless number of ways and correspond to endless fresh impressions and sensations whose most typical is a sort of dismissal or devaluation or (deflation) of the facts which make me go as far as asking myself why, for example, red (the colour) is considered to be red and affects me as red. Why opinions should affect me as opinions and not as pain, why I feel pain, and why this pain I feel without understanding it and which I must continue to suffer so acutely and so bitterly that I persist in analysing it to try and detach it from me, for there is no fundamental reason for what is only a perverse, perverted way of existing and feeling, should cause a condition that makes me so unhappy. No doubt, the rough, stupid way the masses react when face to face with pain in another person, they say "Don't think about it," is right, but it is metaphysically right and does not know it and in no way suspects by what devious paths its sensibility and the consideration of this sensibility would have to follow in the ego's accumulated imagery to arrive at the detachment that other philosophic diction refers to when it says:

"Pain, you are only a word."

All this to end up saying that at times when I have something to say, I am hindered by unnatural haste but the times I have something to say are the exception. Furthermore we would have to stop viewing thought as intellectuals, as if the object of our every thought should be a piece of writing. Only this would not stop one thinking in a singular way, that is to say, essential, better selected than others.

But the condition defined is not a hindrance to expressing oneself and contrary to what you may think, Dear Sir, thought is the thing which is really attacked and personality and being even more so than thought, for not only must I constantly search for what I think about such and such a point and about ideas I am most keen on, but I am so disturbed I often happen to be rendered incapable of interpreting the simplest impressions, or evincing my own way of reacting to the weather, for, example, however incredible this may seem. If it is cold, I may still say it is cold. But it also happens I cannot say it: this is a fact, for something emotional is decayed within me and if asked why I could not say it, I would answer my inner feeling about this fractional, harmless point does not correspond with the three short words I would have to say. Hence this faulty connection between physiological feeling and its becoming conscious, emotionally on the one hand and intellectually on the other, as far as it is roughly possible to summarise and synthesise this series of swift, almost instantaneous, operations which should result in this truism: *it is cold.* Since this faulty connection does not select its subjects or take care over anything, when it spreads it results in the enormous difficulties corresponding exactly with—loss of personality. For I hope we can now quite clearly see how this individual is constituted. An inner feeling which no longer corresponds to sensory perception, and though this sensation may apply to real, tangible, nearby objects or suggested, imagined, distant ones, brought forth by memories or artificially built up, the result is the same, it results in the suppression of all inner life. Sound logic applied to overworked subjects or to a total objective loss can only be invalid and shorn of effectiveness. But, on the other hand, this Cartesian description of the functioning of the mind is as elementary as it is incorrect for such invalid logic would begin by not *extending itself.*

It still remains that I am without ideas or feelings on points which interest me most, simply from the standpoint of my normal personality, great, constant fatigue physically composed of a sort of pain, obstruction located at the spot where the mind summons itself, or more simply obsessed by an awful feeling of emptiness unable to call up any ideas or images. Furthermore, I know that each time I would like to call on my own mine of intellectual memories, I would first run up against this obstruction and after this any comparisons would be impossible.

I must insist on this illustrative fatigue. It clearly expresses the lack of ordinary vitality which prevents me following up my ideas and at the same time stops me reviewing my opinions and judgements at will, preventing me from analysing deeply along with others.

I have lost all comparative standards, all my relative feelings for good and evil, for good or bad, materially and qualitatively!!!

APPENDIX

EARLY POEMS

THE MYSTIC SHIP

The archaic ship was lost in oceans
Afloat with my wildest dreams,
Its towering masts merging
In the vapours of a Biblical, Psalmodic sky.

Pastoral Greece never softly[1]
Played in the bare yards;
The Holy Ship never sold its
Precious goods in exotic lands.

It never knew the hell-fires of worldly havens,[2]
It knew only God, eternal, alone,
It parted infinity's glorious billows.

The tip of its bowsprit dove into the Unknown;
Each night, the Polar Star's pure mystic silver
Flickered at the apex of its masts.

(1913)

Variants

[1] Mysteriously, among the bare yards
An air will sound but not ancient pastorals;
The departed ship never sold.

[2] It never knew the sorrows of the world's havens
La Criée—Marseilles—No. 15, August 1922.

TO A DEAD POET

Alas, his poetic soul had left him
On an evening's macabre sounds and music;

And wonderfully, the sun's yellow hull
Listed among the black shrouds.

So, in my sadness, I had come to see
The remains of this godlike man; to see
Beauty wherein brilliant, flowered, Sublime Thought
Fashioned itself like an altar.

The ocean's music clamoured like crowds,
The rigging rasped like surging seas,
Among the weeping candles' golden flames.

Voices arose from the velvet and gold,
From this great ark processions decked,
With soft tones sounding the flutes of death.

(1914)

IN DREAMS

At the bottom of the garden of our dreams
Finer than our finest genius' dreams
Seized by strange harmonies,
Genius dreams will burst out in us
And lying verse,
Whose endless strophes we listened to
  In dreams.
The wind will bend the trees double,
Trees more sumptuous than sunset,
With fruit of purple, gold and diamond,
With enticing shimmers
With eyes like mysterious emeralds
Emitting mysterious flames.
The wind will contort the trees,
Our bodies will tear inmost music from the woods,
Our voices will vent sublime music
At the gates of wild forests, from high peaks
  Into golden streams.
In order to grasp the spirit of our spheres,

Spirit of night, of decadence and twilight,
Great spirit of darkness and creation,
We will follow the blue path leading
  Straight to eventide.
Streaming forth magnificence and harmony
Like a rosette in a vast oratory's centre.
There we will hear the immortal cadences
Of rhythmical lines and bodies,
Of perfumed Gothic balustrades,
Of the softness of bodies beloved
By men with great, cadential hearts,
  By perfumed poets.

ENO

(1915)

Demain. No. 81. August–September 1920.

EVENING

The pink rivers flowed under the great stars
When all day's rosy doves
Had not abandoned her balustrades
Where women spread their hair like veils. . . .

The golden dragonflies had dropped into the grain,
Harvesters scythed off their wings like heads,
Harvesters of shadows and pink night
With hearts singing like starlit violins.

The evening was flowered with mystic doves
Alighting, dreaming on the heart's urns,
Like golden doves of Eucharistic sacrifices
On the Lord's tabernacle.

The evening was favoured by cradling,
Religious August winds when crickets sing;
An ancient evening when God's soul crumbles,
Reels among the shivering bluish foliage.

(1915)

Demain. No. 83. January–February–March 1921.

BLACK GARDEN

Now they have blossomed forth from the land of death
Those flowers long dream toils poured forth,
Along with ashes and substanceless smoke
From a floor of darkling irises, shedding
Like the hours of darkness, one after another
Into the currents of the terrible, final,
Black water season. The slow diamonds
Of that luminous hour shone, strange
Illuminations of the capsized sun.
The lilies dispersed, the lovely garden's
Dark collection[1] combed by the tide
And the wrought metal of your holy pillars
Quivered, O stems. Night now gives
The master key of its horned portals
To the discharge of freed souls.

Variant
[1] Shadows overflowed the dark collection.

FIRST SNOWS

See this day, so soft, so fine, so pale,
Dying on white secrets:
This expiring day seems human
Sadly shedding its rings in the room.

We feel contented knowing objects,
Like us, drink down this transparent shred,
Flying with us towards the quick clouds. . . .
Time rings its knell on the silent stained glass.

In the evening freshness, branches bewail,
At times a bird dies on the paths.
Then the sky assumes a watery hue . . .
Sister, our love is snowing on the leaves.

Written by my own hand. 18 February 1921

THE BAR

There will still be shabby little bars
With Far Eastern Spices
To harbour the New Year.

Little bars with fabled sailors,
Whose pipes consume old poisons,
Bars buoyant, smoke-filled
Little bars vanishing in the clear dawn.

Bars where the sun and its wake revolve
In the deep red lacquer of the glasses;
Bars with lively tables and dead windows,
Where academic noses will never venture.

For there are other poisons to corrode
The Tree of Life, of our near-budding fibres.
There are wines, strong as disaster,
Not secreted by earthly vines.

I salute you, O bar, freeing us from poisons
Misery, pain and alarm,
By casting us up, naked-souled,
On untormented shores.

Silence preserves you, protecting us, a cold
Silence where medicine never strays,
Silence healing us with prescriptionless, lawless morphine.

EVENING HARMONY

The priestly woods embroidered the horizon,
Where the evening light relit its red lamps,
Along the forest curtain where a thousand branches stir,
Strange visions combed their hair.

A woman appeared, opal and sard
Adorning her coat as purple as the sky;

Her eyes shone in the blue gold of her light hair,
Priestly flowers with supernatural fire.

A coaxing dream with divine-fingered hands
Wept so slowly, the black woods
Called beyond the heavenly hills,
Those Queens resting on the evening's balustrade.

A stronger wind wrung the woodland manes
Waking the skies from sonorous depths
And the voice was lost like dawn,
Erasing the rings on her fingers in veils of day.

On imaginary evenings perfumed with legend
The huge bristling of golden cathedrals
Raises its clamorous woods on lonely heaths.

The translucent stained-glass, still coloured
By fleeting rays of a discoloured day:
Out of the depths of sombre vaults allows
The blue radiance of mystic beauty
To rise in them.

The ashes of night slowly bank up
About dark gates emitting holy incense,
While candles run in the choir's shadows.

The plain is darkened by night's advance,
The trees which determined the solemn outlines
Now sleep in the agonizing silence.

Demain. No. 85. July–December 1921.

THE BOTTLE AND THE GLASS

The absinthe's green lava submerged
The fine evening held aloft by its boughs,[1]
Making stars of an inner, lighter day
Rise in the calm-waved bottle.

Variant

[1] The fine evening held aloft like a wreath

In the bar's mirrors, where the moon snowed
Flows the fountain in the square,[1]
Where the motors of fleeting cars
With frosted eyes turn over frenziedly;
And in the absinthe's green waters,
Enticed by winter and snows
Of their beautiful deflowered bodies,
I stick to madly following
Women love has transformed.

Variant

[1] A sad park's basins ring

VERLAINE DRINKS

There will always be whores on street corners,
Shells washed up on the blue evening's stellar shores,
Belonging neither here nor on earth
Where the wild-sharded cabs whirl by.

Whirl less than in my muddled head;
The absinthe's green stone in the bottom of the glass
Where I drink to the Lord's future perdition and thunder,
Roasting my naked soul.

Oh! how the streets' tangled spindles reel
And weave intertwinings between women and men,
Just as a spider would spin its web
With the thread of people recognised.

MYSTAGOGICAL

The onxy of the dead landscape with its fallen leaves
Was concentrated in the glistening shell;
Then the storm's big drops fell
Reverberating in the caves of night.

But the quivering of the tainted stones
Reminded me of the frozen silver of open heaths;
Every stone consists of a thunder-clap,
Whose power grows latent and transmuted.

And the abyss of sounds rendering their crystal,
To the slow cracking of the casings of stones,
Strips this casing and enters the earth,
With a noise drawn out like an enamelled hair.

MADRIGALS

FLORENT FELS

When the Bishop died, the Devil appeared.
An old devil who frequented poor brothels,
Where accordions evoke the Provinces,
Whose colour sprawls across lost almanacs.

Tell me, did you see that good devil
Looking like a bonze who had shucked off China
Then burnt his old junk
In the embers of the Ultimate calumet.

GEORGES GABORY

Endymion blowing the coral horn,
Each note revealing an ancient asphodel,
Lingering in the forest of evil preparing
A tune to turn all the girl's heads.

ROBERT MORTIER

A house, then another house—all white.
With a pink dirt road,
The whirling of the sun laid bare,
And in the distance, the frayed-silk hills.

In the falling star's plane,
A hill, and in the distance an old steeple spire,

Over there, an old steeple all naked and twisted
And a daisy—hope in a passerby's hand.

MARGUERITE JAMOIS

Like a lily in the heart of a deserted cloister,
Around which ancient silence warbles,
You rock, my sister, to a thinking silence,
In the silence you spread here below.

SIMONE DULAC

O princess flanked by a thousand piccaninnies,
Your finery is composed of talisman stones,
But your heart overflowing with prolific charm,
Consumes us with other rays.

GÉNICA ATHANASIOU

The wonderful night chirping with stars,
Which contemplates us from the centre of the Empyrean,
Are not the equals of your milky complexion,
Nor the lunar flowers of your topaz eyes.

CHARLES DULLIN

In the deathly garden struck by lightning,
You are this fig-tree muttering low,
This black, burnt fig-tree muttering, looking back
To old torments descendant from forgotten times.

You are this fig-tree devoured by lightning,
Whose face is marked by thunder's claws,
Old wizard fig-tree ravaging the earth,
With the ploughshares of your emasculated roots.

The Bottle and Glass, *Verlaine Drinks*, *Mystagogical* and *Madrigals* were published in 1921 in a special number of *Action*.

THE ANTARCTIC

The accumulated grottoes are watered with crystals
Pierced by the bowsprits with their fiery tips,

And the dismasted sails strike plants
Mirrored by reflections in the sparkling waters.

The hulls full of echoes mock the billows
With veiled voices at cavern's beards.
The waves criss-cross the ice; coral
Slowly covers the bottoms of their hulls.

A slow murmuring arises in the cables.
Coral speaks in the bowels of the dead ships,
Cold music congeals in their veins
And light gives rise to yet another sound.

CLOCK

I am not a grim reaper, whatever they may say.
The moon, my betrothed, sits on my knee,
The gloaming rings in some secluded spot,
Behind the hill's painted screen,
Under the green palms of the empty sky.
I am inclined to think it is no doubt
To regulate the slow infusion
Of doubt's darkened wine better,
Along the infinite paths of the criss-crossed skies,
That this stone, this sound stone, is dropped
Into waters of silence, waiting and doubt.

The Antarctic, Clock—Action, No. 10. November 1921.

HARBOUR BAR

to Roland Tual

At the hour the boatman raps on his rope,
Sailors lost in a misty dream
Make their pipes glow red at the door of the little bar,
Bakers are about to bake lunar breads
And I, under the dew falling from aloft,
From the great ceiling stuffed with lice,
I breathe in a whole cargo of late stars,
Caspar's as well.

The Artful Dodger fell asleep amid the shells
Took the last train, slept until morning,
And the entire harbour moved between his hands
The queen who wanted to save me from wreck,
Her two ears wherein shells sang.
The brig battered them at daybreak.

AQUARIUM

In the blue-coloured water which
The golden-day laburnums die with a miraculous soft
  metal,
A great ship raises its vertiginous masts
The watery depths embrace; the day fans
What is left of daylight. The heavens are tired of colouring,
Colouring and shading the flounces
The ship carries tied to its masts,
Staining the bitter waters with dies,
Wrenched from the surface of the migrant day.
This makes the waters ill, the day cold
And troubled, and thus, like in a dream,
Makes the great ship appear wildly extended
In the accumulated waves.

Harbour Bar, Aquarium—Action, March–April 1922.

ST. FRANCIS OF ASSISI'S POEM

I am the saint, I am he who was
A man, insignificant among other men;
With only a few garland thoughts
I vent with a confused sound.

I am this eternally abstracted self,
For ever walking beside its own way.
One day my soul's departed, the next,
I will awake in an ancient city.

I tell you I am the wanderer come
To offer you this humble example's sight.
Thus I left myself one Sunday long ago,
Following the angelus' evangelistic flight.

Now I came to pass into a circle of spirits
Racing down a ring of little hills;
The grass psalmodied all muted
By the asses' hooves bearing spirits smiling on me.

I am no longer ashamed of my robe or my hands,
That belong to me and belong to you, brethren;
That same day I unfettered myself from the world,
The waves passed through my crystalline body.

A city of rigging is spread about me,
Their ramparts like waters of vast seas,
Here I found what begins
And the final word and the after world.

I have only a waxen face and am an orphan,
However, where I am going, Angels appear,
Showing me the way of the strange Father,
Whose heart is warmer than a human father's heart.

Seek me out, I came from the Kingdom of Peace,
That peace penetrating the very stones;
How sad I am at this incessant dust
Of human bones returning to the scorched earth.

I am he who can dispel the terror
Of being a man and going among the dead;
For is not my body the miraculous ash
Whence the earth is the voice through which death speaks.

La Criée. Marseilles. No. 18. November 1922.

THE TIDE

In the endless prolongation of the tide,

Beneath the swelling sails, we hear[1]
Heaven's sails filling the shadows
With the palpitation of expanded stars.

The wind blowing in the diamond cavern,
Where the Madrepore-tree crystal sweeps round,
Will make the unhoped-for enamel of another firmament,
Turn at the colourless threshold of our pores.

I want to plant my living pen here,[2]
So it engraves sea mirages on your sparkling faces,
The sigh which restores your[3]
Freedom in the pastures of my blood.

Variants:

[1] We will hear the sails endlessly belly out
The heavenly murmurs spluttering on the main
With the palpitation of expanded stars

[2] I want to plant my polychrome pen here

[3] Sea mirages, the sign which gives you

MARINE

The ships are falling asleep in the belated harbour,
The smell of dying day slips along the sails,
We see new space being opened up
In the sapphire heavens cradling the stars.

The dark, dumb sea disturbed the glaze,
Whose shimmering crosses the silence;
The town sways between the sails,
With the sluggish movement of birds.

A confused rocking stirs the rigging,
Amid a vague harmonica's acrid sound.
In the smell of the flowing of foreign wines,
The whole harbour falls asleep in a vast mirage.

I do not love you but you still came,
The trees will shake their leaves on our hearts,

We will erect the disillusionment of our former frankness
Towards our pale foliage.

Some part of the wind, the World-wind,
Will reverberate in the vespertine boughs;
Where heaven's grotto will revive its billows
Under the scattering of coral leaves.

The invisible wizard who troubles the air,
Will direct their dance with calmed fingers;
The smell of evening will rise from the earth,
You will love me, I will think I love you.

The sidereal night will arrange its flames,
About the faint globe where days are shed;
In the soul's grotto we will extinguish
The consuming blaze of living without love.

EVENING

At this hour we see the willows bow down,
Night waters receive them in their deep waves;
The bell then rings on the church of worlds
Like the sound of a snowing angelus.

Ships on the sea set their pink sails,
The rosette sheds in the shadow of the steeple,
In distant skies, scattering, we see
The drifting petals of the celestial rose.

Evening's ancient soul leans over us and
With assuaging palms and boughs,
  Finally frees our souls
  With its sweet angels.

The Tide, *Marine* and *Evening*—*Mercure de France*, 15 December 1922.

AN ANTHOLOGY OF DR. TOULOUSE'S WORKS

"ON THE TRACK OF PREJUDICE"

Texts chosen and collected by Antonin Artaud

Preface by Antonin Artaud

Progrès Civique Editions, 5 rue de Dôme, Paris XVI.
u.d. (Paris—1923)
Selections in six parts—each part is entitled "First tableau" up to "Sixth tableau".

PREFACE

Public taste is generally inclined towards ornate work. But the thinking man learns by experience that no composition, especially one of thought, can be undertaken unless it is from the ground up. Dr. Toulouse's work, which was bold from the first, fulfills this condition above all.

Some things must be got rid of. There are distortions in thought, mental habits, in short, vices, which pollute men's judgement almost at inception. We are born, we live and die in an environment of lies. Our teachers and those to whom we were closely linked by blood-ties were bad advisors, we must admit, not consciously, rather unconsciously, by inherited habit.

These are the vices and distortions, vices by nature and vices in practice, those toxins of our mental activity the world generally calls prejudices which Dr. Toulouse has tracked down, right into their last and most cunning lairs. The applications of thought come after thought, after the form and nature of thought. Dr. Toulouse would not have been a complete thinker if he had kept to those essential vices. To hunt prejudice down is an excellent task but fulfilment comes from redressing the prolongation of social and moral wrongs.

Dr. Toulouse's whole life has been one long struggle. His work is like the aesthetics of thought in its total application. For this reason, after an anthology of prejudice, the reader will, if he remains faithful to us, see a series of these anthologies of Dr. Toulouse's work appear in succession, dealing with questions capable of interesting the social and mental life of the times.

MAURICE MAETERLINCK

More than anything else, Maurice Maeterlinck's name evokes a certain mood. This would also be a good way of summing up his contribution to the fields of literature and thought. We will not try to establish that his birth at Ghent, 28 August 1862, bears any relation to the intimate nature of his thought. Maeterlinck had a Nordic soul, which is simply a fact, nothing more. We should consider his talent rather as the result of his soul intensely aflame in the particular tone of the period when he was born and which his poems best define.

A deeply symbolist spirit truly exists in his little book, *Hothouse Blooms* (1889). The other symbolists included and worked up a sort of concrete bric-a-brac of objects and feelings their period *loved*, but Maeterlinck brings out its very soul. Symbolism was not just ornamentation to him, but a profound way of feeling.

In a similar way to the divine Max Elskamp in his *Praise of Life*, all too neglected these days, but with a more *personal*, less orthodox mysticism, Maeterlinck uses certain thought patterns whose *relevance to the present day* is not remarked on enough. A certain method of fusing—by virtue of whatever mysterious similarities—things and feelings, and placing them on the same mental level, while avoiding the metaphorical, is to be found at the basis of ultra-modern poetic theory.

Jean Schlumberger used flippantly to ask how many of his puppet plays still remained. Should we name them in order? In any case some, like *Pelléas and Melisande* and *The Death of Tintagel* provide equivalents in the realm of the mind to the *puppazzi* of the *Commedia dell'Arte* in the realm of movement, and produce an unfamiliar note. Maeterlinck increased his circle of mystical *puppazzi*. He added new faces to his delightful creations. His theatre soon became a whole world where the theatre's traditional characters reappear, evoked from within. With Maeterlinck, the unconscious fatalism of ancient drama becomes the mainspring of the action. The characters are puppets, moved by the fates.

But the intimate bent of his nature led him to seek food for thought among the mystics. He translated Ruysbroek the Superb's *The Spiritual Espousals* (1891) and Novalis' *Disciples at Sais* (1895). Maeterlinck spoke in glowing terms of Novalis, Ruysbroek and Boehme and his ideas make sense, they add new depth to a subject.

In *The Treasures of the Humble* (1896), in the pages consecrated to the thinkers, we discover his fondness for the guiding principle of everyday drama. Maeterlinck had a splendid gift for language, but his thought cannot be analysed. The whole of his philosophy rests in his gift for revealing hidden feelings and unknown connections in thought by the use of imagery.

In 1898 he wrote *Wisdom and Destiny*; in 1902, *The Buried Temple*; 1903, *The Double Garden.* Maeterlinck widened the field of our feelings, he made us sense the movements in the obscure life of plants, the occult laws of natural phenomena.

The Life of the Bees dates from 1901. The anguish, desires, repulsions and ecstasies of these splendid insects are extolled by a lyricist, probed by a philosopher.

Should we also say, like others, that as a philosopher, above all Maeterlinck served as a populariser? No. Maeterlinck clarified a lot of obscure points and moreover he *brought them to life.*

He makes problems pass effortlessly from an imaginary state to reality. He lays them bare and shows them to us alive. First of all he frames them as problems, then isolates the data, giving us the impression of living them, for he evokes them with that modicum of positive sensuality which clings inalienably to our thoughts. Maeterlinck's whole philosophy should not be thought of as contained in the main theme of day to day drama. One would not be a major philosopher for having remarked that the whole of life was this immovable drama wherein the dark contacts between the forces of the fates is woven. Where Maeterlinck is really great is in analysing these contacts and determining their conditions.

Maeterlinck evoked the figures of the mystics of old for us. He knew how to attune us to the stages of their thought. We really feel we are getting to the heart of the problem with him. "God as a person is unknowable," says the wisdom of the Talmud, "but his ways are expressed in numbers and signs." The majority of men are now insensitive to the nature of these *numbers*, which Maeterlinck set down in concise phrases.

Death, *The Unknown Guest* and *The Mountain Paths* contain the last stages of his great curiosity. In these later works the lofty thought of Boehme and Ruysbroek only remain as the echoes of a former doctrine. *The Great Secret* is like a concise breviary of man's conquests in the field of the Unknown.

Twelve Songs (1896) succeeded in melodically expanding his symbolic view of the world in ballad form.

Maeterlinck made his start in literature with a prose tale, *The Massacre of the Innocents* which was published in *La Pléiade* in 1886. Three years later he was famous. Mirbeau in a warm, enthusiastic article praised *Princess Maleine*. This was in 1889.

Maeterlinck translated *Annabella*[1] by John Ford (1895) and more recently Shakespeare's *Macbeth* which, thanks to him, was produced at St. Wandrille Abbey with Séverin-Mars. Among other plays, he wrote *The Bluebird*, *The Engagement*, *Monna Vanna*, *Mary Magdalene*, *The Burgemeester of Stilmunde*, etc. . . .

*

Maeterlinck's philosophy is like a moving temple, each stone clarifies an impression and each impression is a lesson. In no way does it constitute a system. It has no architecture or form, only size, height and density. The

[1] *'Tis Pity She's a Whore.*

upper regions of the mind have mesas as restful as the widest forest clearings. This is where Maeterlinck carries us along with him. What am I saying? He recreates them to his own use and for *our* use, with the imagery and atoms to which our human organs are most sensitive. Such and such a page on Ruysbroek or Boehme maps out a profound plan of their ideas.

Maeterlinck was very knowledgeable about bees. Every phase of their life is inscribed as a living minute in a vast, intense, electrifying drama with the glorious escapades of the feasts, the buzzing battles, the strident funerals of the fallen.

Drama is the highest form of mental activity. The nature of the most profound things is to clash and combine, to infer. Movement is the principle of life itself. Maeterlinck endeavoured to give life to forms and states of pure thought. Pelléas, Tintagel and Melisande are like the perceptible figuration of these fair-seeming feelings. A philosophy emerged from these contacts and Maeterlinck attempted later to *express* it, to give form to the main thesis of everyday drama. Here fate unleashes its whims, there the rhythm is mental and rarified. We are at the very eye of the storm, in circles as static as life.

Maeterlinck was the first to introduce the manifold richness of the subconscious into literature. The imagery in his poetry is arranged according to principles which do not occur in normal consciousness. But in Maeterlinck's poetry, things have not yet been restored to the state of being purely and simply things, things handled by real hands, and feelings remained literary. This was the ransom of twelve centuries of French poetry. But the moderns stemmed the tide.

Maeterlinck appeared in literature at the right moment. He was a symbolist by nature, by definition. His poems, plays and essays are like the different states and shapes of one single thought. The intense feeling he had for the symbolic meaning of things, their secret communications and interferences, resulted in a preference for resurrecting them again, by clarifying them. Thus Maeterlinck interprets himself with the very ideas which serve as his sources.

A Populariser? No. A poet, or rather, a *thinker*. Animator of appearances. A wonderful interpreter, a creator. His thought, which ranges from undefined pantheism (one might call it the physical form of his natural mysticism) to modified spiritualism, ended up after a few deviations, concentrating on itself. It multiplied, embellishing itself with its own insight. The frame is discovered through life. What other illuminations does Pascal provide except for what we might call *inner* illuminations, which leave the unknown in darkness and silence but delve down within the known, within the feasible, unearthing new possibilities. Thus Maeterlinck reduced the extent of the membrane. Very deep truths of this sort are only separated from the highest truths by an insubstantial membrane which man's mind will certainly pierce one day.[1]

[1] Preface to *Twelve Songs* by Maurice Maeterlinck—*Les Contemporains* Series—Stock, 1923.

THE HEAVENS AT BACKGAMMON[1]

Winding organs, little organs, angels,
Inks, lacquers, incredible mixture
Of sharps and sweets;
Go, close-chaptered, my book,
Where the mind's essence is inscribed, divided
Between angels, lacquers, inks and mixtures,
O lucid nightmare, clarified suffering.

MONKEY ORGAN

The hurdy-gurdy teases the monkey
On the narrow-cobbled square,

[1] *The Heavens at Backgammon* appeared in the Galerie Simon's editions in May 1923, with woodcuts by Elie Lascaux.
Catalogue:
In the following, a man is simply trying to express his feelings, only being satisfied when he has reached his true zenith. He puts aside neither feelings nor higher relationships, nor domination of the mind. He incorporates his feelings and their value in the poetic density around them, in the quality and force of the impetus he has given them. Above all, he has sought to lose himself in his poems and the reader along with him.

And the fair surrounds them
Like an unfurled banner.

The old fair rings the skyline
On the edge of the hilltop town,
At every instant the organ bursts out
With a noise like thunder.

A lively waltz
Fires the canvas town,
Some unknown rocket
Shoots through the organ's bowels.

O secret, plausible,
Scaly town, town of roofs,
Receiving the music, intoxicated
By it, you probe it.

Shaking it, without imbibing it,
O music, cutting music
With your harmonic marble,
Crushing the frozen sky.

SNOW

Obsessed with snow, pearl,
Branches stone fire ornament,
White elder pith, virgin wax,
And sperm finally completing the circle.

Mental Plains, fiery coaches,
Fleshen panes, highways of souls,
Ember bellies, flaming breasts,
Virgin husbands, Father Time.

Affected laughter, naïveties,
Frozen flames, indifference,

Restitution, levelling,
Inexpressible purity.

Swirls of souls, white atoms,
We are now a landscape again,
Burning silvers, wise men's souls,
Stolen stars, flying minds.

Boiling signs, ravenous lips,
Delightful conflagration,
Weeded lillies, snow of years,
And this wheel ecstatically turning.

PRAYER

O grant us embered heads,
Heads burnt by heaven's lightning;
Lucid heads, real heads
Crossed by your presence.

Make us born in inner skies,
Riddled with raining chasms,
Let dizziness pass through us
With an incandescent claw.

Satisfy us, we hunger after
Inter-sidereal disturbances;
O pour us out stellar larvae
In place of our blood.

Cut us loose. Separate us
With your cutting ember hands,
Open up these burning roads
Where one dies beyond death.

Make our brains reel
In the depths of their own knowledge;
Ravish our intellects
With the claws of a new typhoon.

LOVE

What about love? We must wash away
This hereditary filth
Where our stellar vermin
Continue to loaf.

The organ, the organ grinding the wind
And the furious ocean's surf,
Are like the empty melody
Of this disconcerting dream.

Of her, of us, or of this soul
We sat at the banquet,
Tell us who are deceived,
O inspirer of the infamous.

She who sleeps in my bed
Sharing the air in my room
Can cast dice on the table,
The very heavens of my mind.

TRAPPISTS

Trappists, trappists cheating heaven,
Swine brother you excrete,
Your pigs reveal themselves as cherubs
In a state of grace.

An essence, a wind come from an unknown place,
Wafts over the dung,
Where the cabbages of the little
Lawnless garden are transfigured.

Through mansions, muddy
With their plenary humility,
The monks lay their dust.
They are vile, they are brilliant.

Manure encloses the secret
Of the planetary diaphragm
Picking up the stuff
Of their overstretched dreams.

Here come hyper-space,
The sanctified executioner,
The slut in a state of grace,
And the frozen-bellied widow.

BALLAD

Music comes out of the windows
Melt, marrow in our bones;
The whole town falls backwards
In a spasm of delight.

In the dark town, the noise
Made by the hard handle turns
Of a few obscure hurdy-gurdies
Increases, increases with every jolt.

Oh! the town is fed up to the teeth
With this nonpareil liquor,
Flooding in through its ears
Piercing it with crystals.

Silence lies at the heart
Of the intoxicating melody
The entire waiting town gleans
From the deep organ's hub.

The waiting is reiterated
In the interval between each rise
The false-hearted handle
Imparts to the clear music.

What Araby or Africa
Holds the tune we are searching for,
Break our vitreous foreheads
O music, wounding music.

THE ORGAN AND THE VITRIOL

The moment is auspicious for the organ
The winds sew in the night,
The organ fills the little square
With its petrifying rhyme.

You smutty little town,
Put a woman on every balcony,
This manna rising from the stones
Is better than your thrills.

I invite prowlers chasing the night,
And mindless adolescents
To black reunions
Spouting out the acid wine of noise.

Those too, seeking words,
In their daedalian dreams,
Those too, seeking their mothers
Asleep beside them.

Sperm and sacerdotal town,
Town whose beds overlap in the sky,
I even invite your church angels
To the sexual feast.

MOON

Bitter tasting tonight,
Jealous of some obscure tart,

Dark, cavernous, dirty with clouds
Floating between the moon and us.

Rancorous moon on the sea,
It was a cheerless moon,
Like a sick man's thoughts,
On the nature of the universe.

In the fabled dark
Where the moon had risen,
Summer's calm
Stretched out its hazy foliage.

FOR LISE

For Madame Lise Deharme

I want to make a human being
Shout out under your violet ring,
Whose cries will set your poetic heart aflame;

In your huge White ring,
Turning your hand into sleeping waters,
I want to make a captive look
Glisten at last, giving itself at last,
Like an oceanic soul offered up to the first fires
Of the sun benumbed by polar ice.

Finally, in these angry days, the more
To emphasize the soothing of your clandestine eyelashes,
I want to make the morning dew fall,
In the amethyst cavity where a poet, intoxicated
By your lunar soul, ceaselessly murmurs.

Today queens no longer build tiered gardens
Where knowledge and fury can arise
Out of our slowly possessed hearts;

But as a king in by-gone times

Carried a calendar,
His barbarous, tattooed body;
Thus from head to toe,
You, with your eyes, your necklaces, your rings,
You make mirages whirl about us,
Able to stay our hunger.

25 August 1935. Sunday.